THE UGLIER SIDE OF THE

TRUTH

Inspired by true events

SJ STEPHENS, MS

FB live: The Biggest Betrayal of all Time

FOREWORD

This book is based on real-life events. Names, locations, dates, and other identifying information have been slightly altered to protect the privacy of the women involved. A great deal of intentionality has gone into protecting those who need it most. I will never reveal, confirm, or deny the identity of anyone in this book.

What readers of the blog, ***The Biggest Betrayal of All Time, Parts I & II*** are saying.

Qiuana Queen - *"Your storytelling is amazing! Keep going!"*

Tyler D. Roy - *"Girl!! Your writing and storytelling are IMPECCABLE!! I felt like I was right there with you!! I know this was not easy to write by any stretch of the imagination, but YOU DID IT and you did it WELL!!! Your HEALING will come thru telling your story, Luv!!!! Thank you again and keep 'em coming!!"*

Toni Owens (May 26, 2021) - *"This blog thing is new to me (with my ole ass smdh). But I have always enjoyed a good real-life read! I am over here on the edge anticipating part II. Check it out y'all! Great blog, dope ass woman! SJ Stephens can you just write a book already."*

Belinda Rucker Little (May 25, 2021) - *"THIS!! My jaw is still on the floor and can't wait for part 2. SJ Stephens, you never cease to amaze me."*

Danielle Bush-Thomas- *"Girl these men aint...whew*

SJ been there! Scratch this blog write a book sheeeessshhh."

Keena M. Davie - *"Dang!! You really left us hanging. Can't wait for the next part!!! That was deep!"*

FearSlaying Cherry - *"Sooo you have got to be my sister from another mister! The way my life WAS set up I literally can just change the platers in your read. Man! Thank you for bravely sharing so openly!"*

Christine Croft - *"SJ...SJ you almost took me out with this one hunny!!! I thought I was ready clearly I was not!!! It was the kisses, and the picture of the freshly soiled panties for me.. (me Mcnasty) ohhh and the taking of his cellphone...PLEASE DON'T KEEP US WAITING LONG!!!!"*

Bethany Rucker - *"Wow! This was amazing sis. Thank You for sharing."*

Alisha Martin - *"I knew this would be good on so many levels this also was very triggering. Thanks for being transparent."*

Jai R Davis - *"Cuzzin this shit right here."*

DEDICATION

Hey y'all hey,

If you're reading this, chances are you have already read parts I & II of my blog, *The Biggest Betrayal of All Time*, and you have more than likely watched the subsequent roundtable with the same title. First, I want to thank you for joining me on this journey; it has truly been one hell of a ride. For me, there was no hesitation on whether I would disclose this story. I pride myself on transparency, and I knew that by sharing, I would undoubtedly help someone else-and helping is always the goal. So often, we women experience trauma at the hands of the men that we love and are unable to express that pain, usually out of embarrassment or fear of retaliation. This book has been a part of my healing process; it was written for me and no one else. My intention is not to hurt or embarrass anyone involved because I genuinely feel no level of disdain toward anyone—well, except MWB. Everyone else I genuinely empathize with. And because of this, I will do my very best to protect their identities both in and outside of this book.

I've been asked multiple times why I chose to turn this private moment into a "public spectacle" (the exact words used). Well, for me, writing has always been therapeutic. I've kept a journal since my freshman year in college, and I've always viewed writing as my safe space. It's where I am free to express my inner most thoughts, no matter how lofty or how dark—it is the one place I feel free from all judgment. Like everyone else, I've been through stages of life where I was too embarrassed to walk in my truth, where the public opinion of others outweighed my mental well-being. I vowed to never be in that place again. Although I was not involved with him as long as many of the other women, this situation affected me, nonetheless. This was an individual that I trusted, based not only on his words but his actions, and he was someone I respected on multiple levels; so, love or not...the hurt, disappointment, and disbelief were the same. But, in all honesty, I have questioned myself multiple times during this process. Why couldn't I take my L in private as the other women had? Why had I been so personally offended that this monster sought me out knowing the things he had going on? What sign of weakness had I displayed that made me such an easy target for him?

Before I go any further, I absolutely must give praise to the Big Man upstairs. Fewer than two years ago, I was on my hands and knees begging for guidance and a way to simply survive. I was going through a divorce, had lost my job as the Director of a local nonprofit in the middle of the pandemic, and was struggling to find my way. For months, I asked God to show me what I was supposed to be doing, or perhaps what I was doing wrong because clearly, I was doing something wrong. Shortly thereafter, my business, SJS. Business Building & More, took flight and by the end of 2020, I had secured nearly $1,000,000 in funding for nonprofit organizations across the country and released two books. At the very moment when I felt as though I had no way, God provided one. For that, I will forever be grateful and as obedient as I possibly can be.

My babies, LeJon II and LeJon III, it's no secret that everything I do is to ensure that my future grandbabies are set for life—so here we go again, lol. I hope that by watching my journey, you both realize the sky's the limit and that the only thing stopping you from reaching your goals is you. Always do the work and move with integrity, the rest will fall in place.

To everyone who supported me emotionally throughout this ordeal—the phone calls, texts, inboxes, emails, and protection; I could not have managed all the madness surrounding this situation without you guys. Thank you.

A special shout out to my roundtable participants and sponsors (no particular order). The hostess with the mostest, THE Terri Allen (aka THE PLUG and owner of the YouTube channel Them Allens), Tim Gordon (author and owner of Pleasant Management), Lexi Brinker,(faith-based coach and host of the podcast, God + Girl), Sheena Smith (TheRebirthofSheenaCatrail), Jai R. Davis (owner of Nite Owl Treatz), Eric and Keisha Wilson (owners of ERG Art Gallery, EW Enterprises, Kays Kraves, and Klassy Kays Boutique LLC), Ronda Smith Branch (certified well-being coach and owner of Worthy of Well Being Wellness Practice), Deserata M. Hughes (owner of Guardian Angel LLC/G.A.S.S.H. & certified crystal healer), Derk Brown (on-air personality for 104.1 The Beat), Lynetta Wings-Paynes (owner of LA Wings Home Health Care and Cut No Corners Cleaning Services), Dr. Monique Ross (aka Dr. Bae and host of Pure Phuckery—the Podcast) and Chantel Polk (owner of The Hustle Firm). Without you guys, the roundtable would not have been as amazing of an experience as it was. And the group chats and Zoom meetings—BABY!!! I will forever love and support each one of you guys. Thank you for listening to my cries, the advice, and for keeping me laughing. I am forever grateful.

Constance Payne, we may only see each other a couple of times a year if that, but that did not stop you from supporting me every step of the way. The constant check-ins, the text messages, and most importantly the prayers, were very much needed and appreciated. You served as my unofficial spiritual guide throughout this process because somehow you knew when I needed you and were always there. Thank you.

To my Kansas City allies…yooooo…. Y'all know

who y'all are, and I would be remiss to not include y'all. Something as messy as this situation turned into a bond that we will forever have. I will never disclose our connection or repeat our conversations but understand, the space occupied in my heart by your presence is here to stay. But trust me, when asked about y'all, my exact statement is, "I don't know no-fucking-body in KC anymore!" Lol, but of course, we know what this is.

MWB. Thank you for exposing the situation to me for what it was. I just wish your intentions had been pure—one sista looking out for another, but they weren't. You simply recognized me taking your spot and tried to run me away like you had done with others before me. My hope is that one day you truly understand your value and stop settling for the bottom of the barrel and everyone else's leftovers. You have never been his first choice, and most likely you never will be. You are simply convenient and provide the accessibility his narcissism needs to survive. As much disdain as I have for you, I believe that every woman, including silly ones like you, deserves better. You spend so much of your time chasing after foolishness and hurting other women in the name of "love" it is apparent that you haven't discovered what truly makes you happy or your purpose—because this couldn't be it. As you said to me, we have so much in common, and but not for this situation, we could have been friends. I truly believe you are DOPE at what you do (I have a copy of your eBook—it's AMAZING), and I admire the hustle, your ability to walk in your truth and bounce back from controversy. But just like with him, you cannot inspire the masses when your reality is a facade...it's only a matter of time before people see you for who and what you are. And your followers deserve better. So as a public figure, DO BETTER (in my Yuppie's voice).

And lastly, the inspiration for this book, my Yuppie. Although I never envisioned this being the end of our story, I believe God has a way of showing us who's really in charge. For what it's worth, I enjoyed every moment we shared, and I do not hate you. Hell, I don't even dislike you, and I was never mad, simply disappointed. The things you did and the lies you told could have potentially really gotten someone hurt because the old me would have reacted differently. As a man, one of your roles in life is to protect us, us being

11

black women, and you did (and continue to do) the total opposite. You took advantage of the love, support, and trust that was given to you so freely. You put us in situations you knew we would have never voluntarily agreed to, and for that, you are a monster. As a father with three daughters—that the world is aware of— envision them meeting you. If that alone doesn't scare you straight, then I don't know what will. In one of our last conversations, you said to me, "I don't want this to be my legacy," and as someone who started as a fan, I don't want it to be either. So, my challenge to you is to become the man that you present yourself to be. Show up in every aspect of your life, not just the ones that gain you fame or profit. I know me publishing this book makes you feel some type of way but understand, this isn't to hurt you, and I will never publicly disclose your identity—even though you continue to push your boundaries and attempt to get under my skin. I've granted you peace and mercy. Please allow me to continue to do so...you know the alternative.

— SJ aka Big Jiz

The narcissist is your worst enemy,
disguised, at first, as your savior.

Dark disguised as light.

Hate disguised as love.

Predator disguised as a friend.

Lies disguised as truth.

Betrayal disguised as loyalty.

Evil disguised as good.

Apathy disguised as empathy.

Rapist disguised as a lover.

Taker disguised as a giver.

afternarcissisticabuse.wordpress.com

Table of Contents

FOREWORD..1

DEDICATION 5

CHAPTER ONE.. 15

CHAPTER TWO 25

CHAPTER THREE 33

CHAPTER FOUR 44

CHAPTER FIVE 55

CHAPTER SIX 68

CHAPTER SEVEN 80

CHAPTER EIGHT 97

CHAPTER NINE 108

CHAPTER TEN 120

Chapter 1

Years ago, I would have taken this story to my grave, because at one point, my image was everything to me. The thought of being judged or labeled as anything outside of amazing disturbed me. My reputation was important to me in a very unhealthy way. Never in a million years would I have even considered sharing something so personal because the whole situation is embarrassing. Not only does it expose my weaknesses, but also my fears, flaws, and most importantly, the fact that at forty years old, I allowed myself to be manipulated. If I had not been so focused on finding a new husband, I would have caught the red flags sooner. But instead, I ignored them for no other reason than I wanted him to be the ONE.

Slim motherfucking Goodie: six-foot-two, brown skin, salt-and-pepper beard, bald-headed, and fly as fuck is the only way to describe him. Even months after the incident and everything that transpired, I cannot take away how fly this man was. Very simple, yet exquisitely dressed at all times. You know the type of

man whose confidence catches your eye first, and the style is simply the icing on the cake? Yeah, my Yuppie was THAT guy. For months, I watched him on LinkedIn, not because I was flirting or even interested in knowing him personally, but simply because he was dope to me. Born and raised in St. Louis, he was a prime example of overcoming whatever life threw at you. The level of tragedy this man had experienced and overcame were all the things that attracted me to him. From the very beginning, I was enthralled at the mere thought of him.

Still and all, I was satisfied admiring him silently via social media, until one day he messaged me. His message had a simple yet powerful undertone. It read, "I've been watching you. I'm impressed and proud of you—you inspire me, and I would love to get to know you." Our first inbox conversation lasted approximately two hours and ended with a cash deposit via PayPal; my dinner that night in Atlanta was on him. That interaction was very simple yet very effective.

Over the next seven days, we continued to communicate via inbox, as we had yet to exchange phone numbers. Finally, he asked if we could video chat; he wanted to see my face and get to know me better; I agreed. He selected a day and time for our date, told me to have my favorite drink poured, and make myself available to him for at least a few hours. Leading up to the call, we messaged all day about our upcoming "date" and our hopes and expectations of each other. That night we spent nearly three hours together, him sipping his whiskey and me sipping my wine. We laughed, exchanged stories, and asked/answered questions until we both were exhausted.

During that time, we both revealed somber stories of past failures, recent accomplishments, and our proudest moments. His smooth voice matched his fly demeanor, and to describe him as articulate and charismatic would be an insult to his dopeness; he was so much more. The way he drew me into every story with his wordplay was effortless, and at the end sentence, I wanted more. Before we called it a night, I asked him what exactly he was looking for right now, and his response was immediate: "A best friend who will show up and never leave." It was at that moment I decided I wanted to be that and so much more.

On day 10, I traveled 247 miles to see him for the first time. Although the situation was new, and technically he was still a stranger, there was no hesitation. He was a major public figure and stood to lose his livelihood if he tried anything strange, so I felt safe. On top of that, part of me wanted him to be everything he promised to be. I easily believed his words without verifying his actions because I was vulnerable—dare I say weak. After so many prior disappointments in love, I needed this to be real.

After dinner and a tour of the city, we spent the duration of the evening in the room drinking, exchanging stories, and enjoying each other's company.

The next morning, the clinginess in me began to surface, I did not want to leave. We were too new to each other for me to have ever felt comfortable those feelings, so imagine my relief when he asked me to stay. As elated as I was, after careful consideration, I declined his offer and headed back to St. Louis. Not even a hundred miles into my ride home, he called and said he would be in my city Tuesday so be prepared to spend the week with him.

Before we go any further, let me help you to understand how things were able to comfortably progress so quickly between us. We communicated no fewer than ten hours daily via text, talking, or video chatting. Our days apart consisted of sharing as much of ourselves as we could from a distance. There was never a time of day when he was unavailable to me, and even when he missed calls, he always called back promptly. Out of all the time we spent communicating, the mornings were by far the best. My first message of the day always consisted of words of encouragement and motivation. During these interactions, I ensured him that I would always be his friend first and that patience, understanding, and forgiveness would be given in every moment it was needed. In turn, his morning message to me was always a prayer. Every he spoke morning he spoke peace, productivity, and protection over us both. He assured me that God ruled all relationships, even best friend relationships in the making, so regardless of our outcome, we would be alright. And at the end he would always say, "Win the day, Jiz."

During our second face-to-face visit, I noticed he was constantly on his phone. It didn't matter the time of the day or day of the week, he always had his phone nearby, and it was always on silent. When he would catch me watching him, his response was always that it was one of his children or his job; two things he knew I would never question. Another thing I noticed was the amount of time he spent in the bathroom each morning. Our first time together, I noticed it as well, and even though it was odd to me then, I simply ignored it. But, after spending consecutive days with him and observing the same behavior, I finally asked him what he did in the bathroom for that length of time daily. Phone sex? Texting? I jokingly told him I was jealous and wanted in. He asked why I would question him about something like that and feigned indignation. I explained to him that receiving nudes from someone ten steps away, who isn't even technically supposed to be naked, was the first reason, and second was the length of time he spent in the restroom. I mean, what man spent two hours in the bathroom every single morning?

Let me back up and tell y'all about the time he was supposedly in the restroom using it when I randomly received a nude from him.... On day one of trip two, I sat on the bed scrolling through Facebook when a text came from him moments after he walked into the restroom. Immediately a huge smile spread across my face, and my heart expanded just a little. How sweet was my Yuppie to be texting me sweet nothings from the other room? I just knew the message was him ranting and raving about how much he adored me, how he thanked God daily for connecting us, or perhaps how stunning I looked at dinner that night. However, I was shocked to open the text to not be greeted by his adorning words of affirmation but rather a filtered image of him standing in front of the bathroom mirror wearing only a pair of white Beats headphones, an impressive erection, and a joint hanging out of his mouth. The picture was dope as fuck, but I was shocked and confused at what was going on. He had told me he was going to the bathroom because his stomach didn't feel right, yet, there I was, moments later staring at a professional quality nude photo of him. He came out of the bathroom completely dressed, only to undress and

21

snuggle up next to me. It was then I realized the picture had not been intended for me but, instead, someone else. He hadn't even realized he sent it to me.

But back to the story at hand. He explained that for as long as he could remember, his morning bathroom routine had been the same. He spent time catching up on all the latest news stories, checked and responded to emails, spent at least forty-five minutes engaging with his followers, used the bathroom, took a warm bath (not shower), and conducted his daily hygiene regime. My Yuppie claimed this was a part of his self-care regimen. Mornings were the only time he had to completely focus on himself and organize his thoughts for the day. He stepped closer to me and said, "I am not texting anyone else but you if that's what you're thinking."

This man's ability to be convincing and sincere while telling lie after lie was astounding. Nothing about what he said even remotely felt like the truth, but I wanted to believe him. His cadence was calm and measured, not at all rushed like a liar usually is. His demeanor was gentle and gathered, and he possessed such an air of authority I quickly found myself believing every word pouring out of his mouth; despite knowing better.

Before I could even respond, he thanked me for being so understanding and verbalized his appreciation several times. That night he disclosed that he had never been faithful in a relationship—well, at least not for the past twenty-five years. In fact, he said he had never dated fewer than three women at a time, he simply loved women. He confided that a fear of his was dating one woman and her leaving him; then, he would be alone. And more than anything else, he didn't want to be alone. For hours, we shared tales of love triangles, physical confrontations, domestic violence, restraining orders, and other horrors. As dope as these vulnerable moments were to me, I now realize that he warned me about a future with him and everything he was capable of, but something about the fact that I didn't have to dig or pry for the information comforted me. It provided me with a sense of connectivity to him because clearly, this meant he trusted me. It was this connection that allowed me to move forward with the situation even when he TOLD me every reason not to. Based on the information shared, I should have run, but he seemed determined to do better. Repeatedly, he said he would be a husband before fifty and that once he found the perfect woman, he could and would commit fully; he had done enough of everything else and was ready for a change.

Chapter 2

My first trip to his home was Valentine's Day weekend, and it was unplanned. After an amazing three nights together, we woke up that Sunday morning to a snowstorm and decided I would stay until the next day. Instead of spending additional money on another hotel room (our current hotel was sold out for the night), he asked if I was comfortable coming to his house, and with absolutely no hesitation, I agreed. The weekend thus far had been a successful one, and I was excited to be stepping into his "real" world. Our days had been filled with bottles of his favorite whiskey, my Hennessey, all the St. Louis must-haves (Red Hot Riplets, Rap Snacks, Red Hot Popcorn, and Sundance), and infused treats. In turn, he made sure I had the opportunity to experience some of the things that made him love Kansas City so much. We spent our days drinking at after-hour spots, sightseeing, restaurant hopping, and visiting all his favorite places. We checked out of our hotel room, stopped to grab coffee and food to go, then headed to his home. When we arrived, he led me up a narrow flight of stairs, and he quickly began to straighten up. He put things in place, threw some things away, and moved items out of my sight; nothing about his actions seemed suspicious. I have a cleaning company that tends to my home, but if I didn't, and someone were to pop up on me, Lord knows the names they would have called me in the group chat regarding my cleanliness; so, I fully understood. As he swiftly moved through the modest four-room space, I sat in the living room contemplating what my being there meant for our relationship? From day one, he told me although he had situations that needed to be wrapped up, no one else mattered, and sitting in his home with him on Valentine's Day was the confirmation I needed.

We spent the remainder of the day doing what had become our norm; snacking, drinking, singing, dancing, and talking. That night we fell asleep sitting side by side on his love seat while watching a movie. At some point during the night, I woke up and realized our positions had changed. I was now on my back in a semi-seated position with my Yuppie nestled between my legs, his head cradled on my breast. I smiled, closed my eyes, and continued to soak up this moment. When we finally woke the next morning, we agreed to a quick breakfast because, as much as we did not want to part ways, I needed to be back on the road before noon. Missouri's weather is unpredictable, and we did not want to risk me being stuck another night.

Fewer than ninety-six hours later, he arrived in St. Louis.

We had not known each other for a full two months, and yet we had spent more time together than apart. What we were doing was more than just dating; we were building. When you are dating someone that you have access to regularly, you may spend three to four hours with them at a time during the courting phase if that. But with us, twenty-four hours was the least amount of time we had spent together, so what may have taken others weeks or months to develop, we did in less than half that time. Our days together consisted of waking up to each other, working side by side, preparing meals together, and dealing with life and family issues together. ...It was just different.

One of the many things I enjoyed about him was that there was nothing he wouldn't do with me. If I wanted to ride for hours listening to music, that's what we did. If I said I wanted to go to the park and walk barefoot through the grass, he was right beside me. The level of compromise we developed with each other was unmatched—it was never simply what one of us wanted; it was always what WE wanted. There was never a moment when he did not do exactly what he said he was going to do for me or with me. When we were not together, we were busy planning the next time we could be. We often discussed the possibility of having more children and me relocating to KC once my son graduated high school. The more we discussed future possibilities, the more I began to believe that the new husband I had been praying for and journaling about had finally arrived.

Then came the conversation about the two other females he was involved with, Queen Sugga and MWB.

Queen Sugga, the university administrator he had been involved with for the past five years, and MWB, the dance instructor he had been involved with for the past three. According to him, Queen Sugga was the only woman he'd dated who had met his family and all his children. She was a beautiful yet simple woman, and he confessed to loving her. They had gone to college together, dated off and on for years, and had developed a strong friendship if nothing else. He described her as trustworthy, laid-back, and hardworking. The only complaint he had with her was that she was unable to have children, and he wanted more.

He referred to MWB as his "good-time Charlie" and said they had met via social media. She was a free-spirited dancer who matched his energy for life and was content with being in an open relationship; for her, a piece of him was better than none. Her only requirement was that she remain his number one. Their relationship had not only been based on mutual attraction but also business; MWB was a social media influencer. She helped him create all his content, established his social media presence, and ran his pages as well. He said he never considered her wife material, but her loyalty kept them together; she was the only one who never walked away. When he finished telling me about these two situations, the only questions I had were 1) did either of these women pose a threat to what we were building, and 2) was he actively still sleeping with them? He promised me they would never cause any issues in our relationship and that he had not slept with either one of them since the end of 2020.

Nothing about us was complicated in the beginning, everything flowed effortlessly. There were no unanswered questions, no spoken doubt or reluctance, and we were locked in on the idea of being together. My Yuppie and I were never in love, but we had the respect and adoration that all great things are made of, sprinkled with a healthy dose of lust. It was amazing. Our goal was to tie up all loose ends and find a way to combine our lives. Even though our plan early on was to be together, there was something about him that prevented me from moving past this initial feeling to anything deeper; maybe subconsciously I knew. But still, he was good to me. He ran my bubble baths daily when I stayed at his house, he cooked and served me home-cooked meals, and most importantly, he listened to me and encouraged me to see what he saw in me, in myself; in his words, that was greatness. Part of the reason I cannot hate him is because of the way he pushed me. We would spend hours discussing upcoming projects and how to monetize our ideas. We discussed the possibility of us writing a book together. We brainstormed on how to monetize our strengths and how to improve our weaknesses. Daily we pushed each other to be greater than the day before; we both saw so much in each other that we were determined to bring it out.

As time went on, I noticed another strange habit he had...spending time in his car. It didn't matter where we were or what time of the day or night—he always found a reason to go to his car. Something was always left behind, or he felt the doors had been left unlocked, or he needed to make a confidential work call and needed to go to his car to do so; it was always something. During one visit to St. Louis, he ran out to his car for a specific notebook he said could not wait until the morning for; he needed it to prepare for work the next day. Initially, the length of time he was gone did not bother me, but once I realized he had been gone for over twenty minutes, I called to check on him. When he answered, he apologized and said he was working; he had received a voicemail from a very important source for a story scheduled to run the next day and the follow-up couldn't wait. The fact that it was the middle of the night on a Sunday struck me as odd, but who am I to judge or even question another's work ethic and methods? After all, I am the chick who works from 7:00 AM to 5:00 PM, naps daily between 8:00 PM and 11:30 PM, then wakes up and works till 3:00 or 4:00 AM; I had no space to judge or question him. That night he was gone for a little over forty minutes, and once again, despite the oddity of this situation, I said nothing.

Chapter 3

The Saturday of my fortieth birthday weekend, he came into town.... I mean, where else would he have been? We visited a local, black-owned coffee shop, did some shopping for both homes at the farmers market, and patronized a few other black-owned businesses. That evening we had reservations for one of my favorite restaurants in town, Bait Stl. As we dressed for dinner, we sang, danced, and took pictures. This was our first-time taking pictures together; he even asked my son to take professional pictures of us. According to him, we were creating traditions, and it was time to start capturing our memories. Dinner was nothing short of spectacular; excellent service, a grown and sexy ambiance, and the menu was to die for. Afterward, we rode around and listened to music and people watching.

It was perfect.

The following day, he brought one of his sons to

my home. I sat in my living room with him and kept him occupied while my Yuppie got dressed-they were headed out for a family dinner. Approximately an hour later, they headed out, and shortly thereafter, I sent him a text message. I wanted him to know how special it was to me that he had brought his baby to my home. According to him, Queen Sugga was the only woman who had met his children...until now.

When he returned to the house, I experienced a side of my Yuppie I didn't know existed. Up until this point, he had only casually cursed in my presence, and I'd never experienced him angry or heard him speak in an elevated tone. Something had gone terribly wrong during dinner, and he was pissed. As he described the incident to me, I could see his anger rising. He went from sitting next to me telling his version of the story to rapidly pacing my living room floor with animated hand gestures and profanity. As he shared the details of the interaction, one would have easily assumed he was talking about a stranger or, even better, an enemy; you never would have guessed he was referencing a family member with whom he'd only had a slight disagreement. I was disturbed at the interaction not only because I didn't agree with the things, he was saying but because as quickly as the situation escalated, it ended. It was as if a switch had been flipped, and he was back to being my Yuppie, composed and calm like the incident never occurred.

A couple of days later, the topic of us being exclusive surfaced again. He was close to having everything wrapped up on his end and wanted to know where I stood. I have always been transparent about my situation; I was still legally married, and although my divorce had been filed, there was no court date so we agreed to revisit the conversation in another month or so. Around this time, something in his life changed, and his behavior was a direct reflection of it. His consistently laid-back demeanor was replaced by one full of erraticism; everything began to annoy him. When questioned, he would also blame the pressures of work, the frustrations of leads not panning out, parents at the games he refereed, everything but me or another woman. The most consistent man I knew and had grown to cherish was slowly becoming someone I did not recognize. On multiple occasions, I asked what was going on and if there was anything I could assist him with, the answer was always no. Despite his refusal to admit that anything was wrong, I could sense that something had changed, I could feel the difference, and it scared me.

One Thursday, after a day of our usual routine—good morning prayers and affirmations, midday check-ins, and evening video chats—he called me around 8:00 PM and said someone had sent something to my inbox. He went on to say that he couldn't talk, his daughter was in the car with him, but that he would call as soon as he dropped her off, that he was sorry, and would explain later.

As I listened to him talk, my stomach dropped, but truthfully, I wasn't surprised. It was almost as though I had been waiting on this moment, and it had finally arrived. As soon as we hung up, I checked my FB messages, and there it was: a group chat had been created by MWB that also included Queen Sugga. Her message read:

Good evening, ladies. We all have someone in common. I am sure Mr. will try to convince you that I am crazy and just a trick, which is fine, and you

are free to make your conclusions. SJ met L, his GF of almost five years. L met SJ, the woman in STL he started a new relationship with a few months ago. Me, I've been around for 3. Oh, and he's terrific to travel with. We've been to Memphis, Dallas, Arkansas, Columbia, STL, and I left Springfield about 6 hours before you arrived in SJ. So enjoy your trip to Nashville next week. Just in case you need actual proof—here ya go. There's so much more, but I think you'll get the point.

(The only thing omitted from this text is his name.)

The message also included pictures of them together over the years, including in the bedroom and screenshots of their recent conversations. The conversations ranged from him acknowledging my presence in his life to him saying that he missed her and would always love her. In one message she shared, they talked about the irony of her and a KC public figure somehow ending up at the same place, at the same time, all the time and he questioned whether she was romantically involved with him. She fired back that he could either cuff her (with a diamond ring emoji) or shut the fuck up because she too found something ironic—this new relationship that he started with me, Big Jiz. The dynamic of their conversations led me to believe that this wasn't their first rodeo.

Before I responded to her, I called him because I wanted to allow him the opportunity to explain. I needed him to make this entire situation make sense. That night, my Yuppie, the Narcissist, was present in his full-blown glory. Even after witnessing the family incident that occurred less than a month earlier, nothing could have prepared me for the series of phone calls and text message exchanges we had that evening. Instead of being somewhat humble and apologetic, he was angry. Angry that she messaged me, angry he had been exposed, and angry that I had questions. I sat and listened for an hour as he became completely unhinged. His first line of defense was that she does this all the time and that she was not to be trusted or listened to. She was diabolical, a liar, and unhappy with her life. Because he no longer wanted her, she was determined to hurt everyone close to him; he admitted this was not her first time reaching out to women he dated. As I listened to his varying explanations of why this lady was in my inbox, I realized, plain and simple, he was lying. Yes, I felt there was a level of sickness to her based on the content in the messages but what couldn't be denied was the fact that he has been engaging with her even when he promised me, he wasn't. There had been days when we were together, and he was texting her as he sat next to me. There was even one incident where he asked to be dropped off at the auto repair shop on my way back home. He said if his vehicle wasn't finished by the end of the day, he would simply catch a cab home. MWB's messages told me otherwise; he had been texting her that entire morning, and when I dropped him off, she had been waiting around the corner to pick him up.

And then there was Springfield. He was scheduled to be there for six days due to work and asked if I would join him at the end of the week. He claimed he hadn't wanted to be away from me for that long. Turns out, while I was there with him Wednesday, Thursday, and Friday, she had been there Monday and Tuesday, and just as she said in her message, she left a few short hours prior to my arrival. I was in complete shock because while he was there with her, nothing about our pattern changed. We still talked and texted as usual, and he shared with me the daily adventures of coaching and detailed every moment of his day for me. From the details of an amazing Mexican restaurant, he found that he couldn't wait for me to experience to the strange dorm setting they expected the refs to share...he couldn't wait to see me and wished I could come sooner. So, to learn that she had been there with him before my arrival was baffling.

How did she get there? Initially, he told me that she popped up on her own because she stalked his social media and knew his location. Eventually, he admitted that he asked her to join him but made it clear that she had to be gone by Wednesday because that is when I would be arriving. My Yuppie described MWB as being a depressed, suicidal maniac, and he felt obligated to spend time with her before cutting her off completely. He was adamant they had not had sex, because after all he would never disrespect me like that. He just couldn't turn his back on her, she needed him.

The more questions I asked, the more defensive he became. He couldn't understand why I would take the word of some crazy chick who was only upset because I was slowly replacing her in his heart. Then he blurted out, "If you're going to leave me, then go ahead and leave. That's what they all do anyway."

After that, the line went completely silent for what felt like forever. I didn't know how to respond to what was just said. it struck me as both odd and disheartening because here was this super confident, damn near egotistical man who had accidentally disclosed one of his many sad truths; he was so accustomed to disappointment and being left that it was automatically what he assumed I would do as well.

<u>Narcissistic personality disorder</u>

(Based on information from the Mayo Clinic)

A mental disorder where exaggerated feelings of self-importance are displayed, but low self-esteem exists. In some cases, NPD can be linked to a person's childhood and is characterized by an increased sense of self-importance and a continued and excessive need for admiration.

The most common signs that someone is a Narcissist:

> *Lack of empathy*
> *Very fragile self-esteem*
> *Has mood swings when criticized*
> *Monopolizes most conversations*
> *A false sense of superiority over others*
> *Overly boastful and often exaggerating one's achievements*

Chapter 4

That night I rode around for hours in total disbelief. I wanted to believe his explanation, as implausible as it was, but deep in my heart, I couldn't. As much as her reaching out to me disturbed me, I knew at the very least that she was being partially honest. Eventually, I responded to her, and in a nutshell, told her to leave me the fuck alone. The mere fact that she and my Yuppie had open conversations about me was reason enough that she shouldn't be bothering me. She knew who I was, so what was her point? I was so disappointed that at her age, not only was she a damn fool but dared to be a bully. Informing another woman of a situation to potentially spare her heartache or to protect her in some aspect is one thing, but that's not what she was doing. And when I noticed that she had also sent messages to my business and personal IG pages, things got slightly different.

For seventy-two hours, I gave her ass the business. At this point, she was watching my story as fast as I could add to it, so I made sure that she saw everything she was looking for. Although I never posted his picture, I made sure that she knew it was him I was referencing. All my captions were about her silly, funny-looking ass, how ridiculous her dye job was, and how much of a buffoon she was for wanting to argue with me over a nigga who had never been exclusively hers. Most importantly, a nigga who chose me. And my Yuppie did nothing to make the situation better. In messy nigga fashion, he added fuel to the fire every chance he got. Every message she sent him, he forwarded to me. Every voicemail she left, he either played for me or sent to me. He was determined to show me that she was not a love interest but rather a sick, delusional woman who refused to let go. He stood on the fact that he wanted only me and was rocking with me one hundred percent and that she was simply trying to destroy what she saw us building; she was jealous. To prove how "done" he was with her, he began telling me all of her business. I was given intimate details about her divorce, the ex who left her for a white woman, and that she had been charged with embezzlement along with her mugshot and the blog she wrote about it. When I asked him why he shared these things with me, he said he was giving me the ammo to fight back; she was just getting started.

In response to the things I was posting, MWB had some tricks up her sleeve as well. For days, she dedicated a whole IG series, every post, and every story to my Yuppie. She posted pictures and videos of them together and talked in detail about the love triangle we were currently in. She proclaimed not to care; after all, she subscribed to the "boyfriend by committee" theory (dating and sleeping with multiple men at once); but everyone could see through her shenanigans; she was hurt.

In hindsight, and knowing everything that I know now, my Yuppie played the shit out of us both. He told us both just enough to make us hate each other but still feel enamored with him. Although frustrated with him, we were never actually mad at him. It was almost as if we both completely forgot that there would have been no us (MWB and myself) but not for my Yuppie. Yes, she rubbed me the wrong way with her passive-aggressive behavior, and as I've said a million times over, I won't be bullied or bothered, however; I was publicly fighting this chick over a man that I did not love and who was proving himself to be a liar every single day. No matter how much she bothered me, the fact was, there were things she shouldn't have known and places she wouldn't have been if what my Yuppie had been telling me was true. And then there was the revelation that I was not the first person she had ever contacted; there had been several before me, most recently in January of 2021, to be exact. So, despite him telling me that he would never forgive her for "doxing" him he had forgiven her numerous times before, so why would this time be any different? I had simply fallen victim to their toxic love cycle.

This incident triggered me to write my first blog. Before this, despite having two published literary pieces, I didn't consider myself an author or even really a writer. I've jokingly said more times than I can count that I am simply a chick who had something to say but to classify myself as an Author was a stretch. To give myself such a prestigious title would be to take away from technically trained writers or those who had earned bestseller status; that simply wasn't me. Little

47

did I know that one blog would be the trajectory change that my career needed. After an exhausting day of antagonizing MWB on social media, I grabbed my laptop and started typing. I never had a plan or even an idea of what I wanted to discuss; I just knew she would be the topic. After typing for thirty minutes and spending another thirty minutes contemplating whether I truly wanted to share this story, I hit publish and walked away from the computer.

Fun fact about me, I rarely read anything I write. I did not read college papers, articles, or grant proposals, and I've never read one of my books from start to finish. Call it arrogance (or perhaps stupidity), but I am confident enough in my writing process and my ability to produce that my habit has been to write something, do a spell check, and send it to the editor (depending on the size of the story) or send it to print. Although I was proud of the blog I had produced, I was nervous to see his reaction. I hesitantly texted him the link. A few moments later, he called me and said, "Yo...that was dope, my Brown Sugga Baby. You are one helluva storyteller."

Coming from him, a respected journalist and a three-time author, this compliment filled my heart. The next few minutes were spent talking about writing style, and suggestions. He even made grammatical corrections on the piece for me.

Why You Hating Outside of the Club? You Can't Even Get in — the Blog

To know me is to know I have grown leaps and bounds over the past few years. From the angry, bitter, mean girl to what I now consider to be the total opposite. I am intentional about how I treat people and, most importantly, how I show up for those surrounding me. It's not because I had some profound life-changing come-to-Jesus moment but simply because I wanted to be a better version of myself, and I took the steps to do just that.

After the demise of my marriage, I was broken. And when I say broken, I mean, "vodka straight out of the bottle with nothing on my stomach for breakfast" broken. Now be clear, my marriage solely did not put me in this place; it was life in general.

You see, I come from a broken home, and despite many years of denial, I had daddy issues. It had been over thirty years since I last saw the man I was raised to believe was my father. For me, those daddy issues manifested around age eighteen when I became a little broken girl who dated older men to fulfill that gap. I was seeking a father figure, someone to provide stability, to love and protect me, but instead, I ended up with old-ass men who had NO business even entertaining me. In hindsight, the shit was creepy, and thank GOD I have a son because I cannot fathom ME being MY DAUGHTER during this phase...

Instead of staying in this broken place, when I returned to St. Louis, I did the work. Two years of counseling, two times weekly, no attempts at a relationship, a lot of alone time, prayer, and meditation.

Bam, the year is 2020, and I am better. I no longer held on to any resentment for anyone. Not my father, whoever and wherever he is. Not my husband, who I technically had every reason to hate. Not even my kids' dad, who randomly popped up with a wife after three months of dating, after telling me for ten years he would never remarry. I let go of everything that was holding me back and focused on me and my children.

I made it through all of 2020 with no issues. No bad days, no tears, just a sense of peace and self-purpose.

But y'all know that thing about the devil, right...his ass is busy-BUSY.

On April 15th, the devil sent his baby daughter to my inbox with the sole intention of hurting me because she was hurt. A hurt caused by someone she loved and trusted, and because of this, she was determined to share her pain. As I scrolled through endless text messages, pictures, and videos, the anger grew—not at the situation but at her audacity. I mean, in 2021, are women approaching other women about men? The whole concept was utterly ridiculous to me.

Little did she know; the old me was DEFINITELY with the shits. Every mean girl bully tendency I had ever possessed resurfaced. I not only matched her energy, but I cranked it up in overdrive. For seventy-two hours, I was the pettiest, meanest, and most immature version of myself. UNAPOLOGETICALLY. For seventy-two hours, all of the peace, love, and light I worked so hard to cultivate was gone. I was back, BABY!!! The Lil ghetto girl from the Horseshoe by way of Berkeley had been given oxygen and was thriving. I relished the fact that she was hurt, upset, and embarrassed...simply because she came for me.

On the seventy-third hour, I snapped out of it. This wasn't me. I was no longer this mean girl with nothing to lose. I am SJ Stephens, the two-time best-selling author. I run my own Grant Writing Academy. My business is POPPING!!! I have clients in thirty-one states. I am working my first corporate job ever, making more money than I could have imagined. I've tripled my income over the last year, and my projections for this year are even better. My kids are amazing. I mean, life is truly GOOD.

So just like that, I stopped. Not because she deserved my mercy or my grace, but because the situation wasn't worth it.

So today's word of the day...YES, everyone,

even the strong get triggered; and that's ok, it's normal, and most importantly, it's life. But when you truly obtain a level of peace, you do not engage in bullshit because it's beneath you in every sense of the word. So, I decided to allow her to watch my page, my stories, send screenshots to him all because I realized...ol' girl was simply standing outside of my club, happy hating, when she couldn't even afford to get in.

—SJ

Chapter 5

I knew there would be push back from her once I published the blog because she had still been watching my page. I knew she would see it, but honestly, I didn't care. My sole purpose was to show her that I was NOT one of them and that if she continued to go low, I was on a fast track to hell; I had no intention of playing fair. While I wasn't vested enough in him or our relationship to stay through thick and thin, I was petty enough to make her feel my presence.

After the blog was released, my Yuppie and I sat together and laughed at her as she slowly began to lose it on social media. Her stories continued to revolve around him, and we got a kick out of it. Although I still didn't trust him, the satisfaction in knowing that she continued to call and text him throughout the day satisfied me and, sickly enough, made me stay. In my mind, I was showing her who the Big Dawg was and plain and simple, that I had won. As she acted out as a child on social media, I continued to bask in the glory, knowing that I would soon be in KC with her most prized accessory on my arm, him.

Almost immediately my inboxes began blowing up with questions, comments, and critiques about the blog. I received anywhere from 10-15 messages daily about the situation, so when I received a message request on IG, I thought nothing of it until I read what it said.

Apr 21, 5:31 PM

Good evening love, I don't know why your tribe isn't advising you differently but you look hella dumb going on and on about the old lady that tried to disrupt your peace and you aren't the one to mess with and you gonna keep being her favorites favorite etc. The amount of energy you are giving to "bashing" makes you look hurt and you are only giving her your power. She did what she did for her peace, not to hurt you or his actual GF of 5 years. You want to feel like you won by "keeping" a man with multiple women, baby mommas and no money? That's your choice. He's a narcissistic leech with nothing but dick to offer who feeds of powerful women. If you took the time you would notice that his three main, including you are bosses in their own right. He's a man child who had you all wrapped up. She broke free and hopefully his GF did too so now he's all yours until he does the same ro you if he already isnt building up his roster.

To each their own. Just leave her be and go be happy with your man whore. Bye boo 💤

Now, if you know me, you know exactly how I responded to this initial message because again, I say, I won't be bullied or bothered by anyone for any reason. Unbeknownst to me, amid this mess, she had sent all of her friends to my page as well. To be fair, I had done the same thing; however, none of my friends ever contemplated reaching out to her, nor would I have ever encouraged them to do so. I could not believe she had someone inbox me on her behalf at her damn age, I was outdone. Before I responded, I called my Yuppie to share with him what was sent to me. The first thing he said was that it read like she (MWB) wrote it and warned me that it was probably a fake page. He insisted that I block her, and everyone associated with her. He claimed they would keep bothering me if I allowed them to. As much as I wanted to please him, his insistence that I block her raised a red flag. Was he really trying to protect my peace and our relationship, or did he want to severe ties between she and I so that we could no longer share information? If we didn't have access to each other, how would we know what was going on with him?

Against his wishes, I responded. Surprisingly, our

interaction was somewhat peaceful, and we gained a better understanding of each other's positions in the situation. MWB was her friend, and she was sick of this toxic cycle she had been witnessing between the two of them for years. Her friend was hurting because of him, and now I was adding to that pain. She wished that we would talk instead of allowing this situation to play out publicly. She went on to tell me how much of a user and a narcissist my Yuppie was and confirmed what I already suspected: I was not the first female that MWB had an encounter like this with. This had been their pattern for the past three years, and as far as she knew, there was never a time when they were exclusive with each other or that she could remember her friend being genuinely happy with the situation.

The friend asked me to call MWB and sent me her cell phone number. In return, I sent her mine and agreed to talk to her whenever she was ready.

The next morning, I received a message from MWB. She started with a humble apology and thanked me for being open to speaking with her. She told me she never set out to bully me and agreed that the tone of her message could have been different but that watching me fall for him made her heart sink. She saw so much of me in her. Yes, it was true, he had been with other women, but this was different; she felt she was being replaced. Her exact statement was, "He was willing to lose me for you. That's when I knew you were a problem."

I felt horrible. I knew the feeling of devastation associated with trusting a man who wasn't trustworthy. Of loving a man who could not love me back in that same manner, and I most certainly knew the heartbreak of watching your person become someone else's. I apologized.

I stressed to her that before her messaging me, none of my posts related to him or things that we were doing had been directed at her. Yes, I knew she existed, but I would have had no way of knowing that they were still intimately involved or that she had been watching my story. In fact, until her message, I never even knew her name. He told me she was someone from his past that he was working to end things with, and I believed him.

During our conversation, she asked if there was

anything I wanted to know, and honestly, there was only one thing; how did she know who I was? The answer provided was not at all what I expected it to be. MWB said back in January when my Yuppie and I met, she noticed that I put a heart under one of his pictures. Because she was the one who established his social media accounts, she knew his patterns and could always tell when something was going on. She went on to say that usually, when a female 'hearts' his pictures or a post, it is usually because he has been in that female's inbox. She had begun watching my page for clues to confirm her suspicions about my Yuppie and stated that she knew everything... the time I spent in Kansas City with him, when he came to St. Louis with me, where I worked, the projects I had been talking about on social media. Despite her presenting the information, he continued to downplay the situation, so she continued to watch; she needed confirmation. She jokingly said that he always refers to her as a CIA agent because she always found out, no matter how hard he tried to conceal his indiscretions. There were three things that she said that stuck out in my mind during this conversation:

1. There was a weekend he was in St. Louis, and we went to Freddie Gs. He knew the owner, and in honor of Black History month, we decided we were only eating at black-owned establishments. In a picture I posted, I did not show his face, but you could tell I was not alone, she knew he was with me because she noticed his wrist in the background. The irony of that statement, he does not have tattoos or anything else distinguishing; she simply knew her man's wrist.

2. My birthday weekend, I wore this super cute sheer dress, so of course, I took a million selfies and posted them to social media. She said that she knew he was in my house because she saw a pair of white Beats headphones on my bed, they had been a gift from her, and she saw his book bag and hat on the floor behind me. Also, in these pictures, she had read the affirmation sticky notes I had taped to my mirror. She was concerned that I was pregnant by him. One of my affirmations was my desire to become a mother in 2021.

3. But the picture that set her off, that let her know she had to reach out to me, was when I posted a boomerang of a new shoe I recently purchased. The

caption read, "Shoe of the day because this weekend we are changing places. Nashville, here we come." My hashtag was #SlimGoodie (my nickname for him).

For her it was one thing for her to know that we were dating, because he never denied that, but for her to witness him doing everything he was no longer doing with her, with me, was something else entirely. Again, I felt bad and found it harder and harder to stay mad at her. She was as much a victim as I was. And the reality of the situation was that he was the root of all the confusion. If I wasn't mad at him, how could I walk around mad at her? I let it go.

My Yuppie was yet again PISSED that I entertained a conversation with her and had no problem expressing his feelings. He ranted and raved for days that she was a psychopath who was only toying with me mentally and emotionally. I told him that our conversation went well and that I truly didn't expect any more issues with her; we were good. He said I was a fool if I believed that. I took what he said with a grain of salt. He was correct in saying I didn't know this lady from a can of paint and who better to know her patterns and habits than him; her lover of three years. But what I know is niggas, and the fact that they will go to any extreme necessary to ensure that their lies are never exposed. He didn't want her to tell me that he had not been trying to break off the relationship with her; in fact, he was the one who reengaged their situation. She had publicly disclosed her dating app hookups and had been seen around the city with another major public figure, and he had become jealous. His reaching out was not out of love or because he was ready to stop being who he was and who she needed him to be, but for no other reason than he didn't want to lose his grip on her.

That next weekend, we were scheduled to go to Nashville (the trip that triggered her), but my Yuppie told me that his children had a basketball tournament, and as much as he contemplated asking their mom to take them; he felt it was his responsibility because he was the one who signed them up. But still, he didn't want to disappoint me. As a mother, I understood his obligation to his babies and insisted he attend the games but told him I still planned to travel to Nashville without him. The day I was scheduled to leave, he called and asked if I would spend the weekend with him. He explained that since the trip was off, he picked up extra hours with his part-time gig, so it wouldn't be our standard weekend. The one-on-one attention I was accustomed to receiving wouldn't happen. But he would do his best and wanted to fall asleep and wake up next to me. I canceled the hotel room and headed to Kansas City.

Friday, when I arrived, we did our usual. We ate good, drank good coffee, liquor, and then he had to leave for his daughter's game. When I drove back to his house, I couldn't believe myself. I was becoming that girl. The ones I talk about and feel sorry for because I often wonder how they could be stupid enough to run behind a no-good man. I couldn't believe that after everything I learned about him, the way he reacted, the arguments, the lies...I still ended up there with him. Once again, I felt like a complete fool. Up until her messages, I had been able to rationalize every odd thing he had done. Him being on his phone consistently, or any of the other small quirks that never quite made sense-running to his car for any and everything, waking up at all hours of the night, and the time spent in the bathroom. But due to past relationship trauma, I had a hard time deciphering between my insecurities and red flags. As a result, I had promised myself I would trust him until I had a reason not to. Well, MWB gave me every reason in the world not to trust him…but there I was still.

He came home straight after the game, and we fell asleep wrapped in each other's arms, no intimacy—he claimed he was physically exhausted, and emotionally, I was drained. Saturday morning, his baby girl's 10:00 AM game was canceled, but he was still scheduled for the part-time job at 2:00 PM. Despite the things that I knew to be true about him, the optimist in me continued to find silver linings around the black cloud he was becoming in my life. Before he left for the day, he ran me a bubble bath, turned on some music, and served me breakfast in the tub. He again apologized for the confusion his past had caused me, and he said he wanted us to start fresh. He continued and said that he knew nothing he could say would make the situation go away, but he was willing to do whatever it took because he didn't want to lose me. In fact, he refused to lose me.

I believed him.

Before he left, he made sure to run and get me coffee and gave me suggestions on activities I could do around the city; he did not want me sitting in the house wasting a beautiful day. I spent my day at the riverfront park, a frozen daiquiri spot, and I eventually went "home" with take-out for us both. Throughout the day, we talked regularly, more than we had in the past when he was working, but he claimed a few games had been canceled, and since he felt so horrible that he wasn't with me, he wanted to check in and make sure I was ok.

Another reason I fought so hard to believe him (even when I knew he was lying) is because amid his bullshit, certain things I couldn't imagine a man with multiple women doing. For example, I had complete freedom to come to KC anytime I wanted, I had free reign and access to his home, and we spent a lot of time out and about the town. A town where everywhere we went, someone recognized him because of his position in the community. We did everything together—visited various restaurants, the riverfront, stores, bars, clubs, there never seemed to be any limit on what he would do with me. He couldn't do that if he had women spread throughout the city, could he?

Chapter 6

On Sunday, he woke up to several missed calls from his family members. Eventually, he got someone on the line, and they revealed that a very important male figure in his life had passed away. The look on his face was a mixture of fear and devastation. To watch him go through such a range of emotions in such a short time had also been a red flag, emotionally he was very unstable—shock, sadness, and devastation quickly turned to fear and then a false sense of strength. I watched his face harden with his forehead wrinkled, almost as if he was scowling. Then he quickly squared off his shoulders, and just like that, my Yuppie was back. It was almost as if, for a split second, he allowed himself to be vulnerable. I'm sure in his eyes, it was a sign of weakness, but to me, it was beautiful. This was a man who had suffered unspoken traumas his entire life; the only coping mechanism he had was to recover quickly. He defined himself as unbreakable.

We soon learned the funeral would take place the day before his birthday, which just happened to be Mother's Day and we were forced to cancel yet another trip. The day of the wake, he made it to the city with less than an hour to spare and went straight there. Truthfully, I had not expected to see him until much later that night. I assumed he would want to spend time with his family, many of them he said, he hadn't seen in years, but he didn't. When he made it back to my house, he was exhausted. I could see the stress and the weariness on his face. I asked if he wanted me to grab take-out and we just chill, or did he want to go out; he said he wanted to go out...that he needed to go out. After riding around for about an hour, we settled on a restaurant in Illinois that he had never visited before. Over dinner, we spent our time comparing schedules because now that businesses were opening back up, we had plans. He was a fan of live music, festivals to be more specific, and there were several coming up that we planned to attend. He was as engaging and charismatic as he normally was, but still didn't seem present. He was going through the motions. Our ride home was silent, and when we made it there, we showered and went straight to bed.

Something didn't feel right about him lying next to me, I couldn't shake this strange feeling, and it was that feeling that kept me up most of the night. I laid there for God knows how long, recapping everything that had happened from day one; the good and the bad, and I had to admit, there had been far more good than bad but, I still couldn't shake this feeling, and it was making me sick to my stomach. I slid carefully out of bed to avoid disturbing him, grabbed his phone, which was at the foot of the bed, and went into the bathroom. I didn't know exactly what I was looking for, but I knew there was something in there that would give me the confirmation I needed to end or move forward with this situation.

The first thing I noticed as I looked through the text messages was that everybody had been assigned a nickname. Although he called me his Brown Sugga Baby, there was another chick in his phone with that nickname, my number was saved under Big Jiz. There was Queen Sugga, Lil Baby 2020, Kesha 2020, DD, and Author Chick, to name a few. I struggled to process what I was looking at.

While going through his messages, I learned that while he was at his family members' wake, he was having simultaneous conversations with me and two other women. When we were at dinner, and he said he needed to go to the restroom, he had placed a call to Queen Sugga. While I was taking my shower, he placed several calls to different women. The information I consumed in such a short amount of time completely floored me. I didn't know what to think or feel. I'd spent the last month mad at MWB for interrupting my peace and my relationship when she should have been the least of my concerns because she was the least of his. Still uncertain of how to move next, what I did know was that I didn't have much time before he realized I wasn't next to him and came looking for me. I couldn't have his phone in my hand, still, I couldn't move. I clicked on the name Queen Sugga whose message read, "Stop calling me. I do not want to talk to you, and I know you are down there with SJ." I clicked on Lil Baby 2020, and his message to her said, "You know what's in the bookbag, what's always in there. Our favorite and condoms. See you when I get home." I clicked on another one, and it was a female saying, "I am sorry I couldn't be there with you, baby. But I love you, and I'll see you when you get home."

At this point, I was unsure of exactly what I was reading but to simply say I was confused and hurt would be an understatement. MWB had warned me that he was a serial cheater and not to be trusted, but this was beyond anything I could have ever imagined. Once again, I felt horrible, although she and I had squashed our differences the fact that he allowed me to spend time mad at this woman and "proving a point" to her when he knew everything else, he had going on hurt my feelings; how could he?

I sat there replaying the conversations that my Yuppie and I had on almost a daily basis. The ones about us being exclusive because I was a wife, not just someone you messed with, and his adamant refusal to step into fifty as just a baby daddy and not somebody's husband, my husband. The constant reassurance that the women in KC stressed him out and him reminding me that he chose me—someone close enough to get to when he needed them, but far away enough that I was a place of respite when life there got too hard. The tales of everyone else being so mean to him and not understanding him and him proclaiming that all he needed was a clean slate and that I was in that clean state. Yet, there I sat, reading messages that proved to me none of what he said to me could have possibly been true.

I'm not even sure how much time went by, but just as I stood up to open the bathroom door, the phone lit up. I quickly sat back down and opened the phone—this time, it was an inbox on Facebook, not a text. It said, "Baby, Mali Music is coming here. Let me know your schedule so I can grab us tickets," and there was a flyer attached. The flyer was one I saw floating around on social media. The concert was here in St. Louis at the Ambassador. It was at that moment I realized; I was not his St. Louis girlfriend; I was simply one of them.

My heart.

I closed the message, stood, and slowly turned the doorknob. I knew I had been in there longer than was safe. I stood there for a moment in the dark to make sure he was still asleep before I tiptoed over to the bed, placed his phone back on the edge where I found it and went to the living room. Everything in me wanted to cry. I was so damn disappointed and felt so stupid. It was time for a candid conversation with God because, to be frank, I was mad as hell. How had God allowed this man to enter my life? Had I not been through enough? Didn't the fact that I prayed my way out of the last situation count for anything? I mean, come on now. I had repented for all my sins. I was tithing faithfully, I prayed all day every day, I was good to people, I showed grace, I loved people, and I supported and took care of people.

Why me?

What was the lesson here? Was it because I wanted it (as in a Husband) too bad, and God was slowing me down? Was there something I had done in previous years that was finally catching up with me? Yes, we had only been in the game for months, which seems like an eternity; but it was never the length of the relationship, it was the quality and the promises. I thought of how rapidly our friendship progressed and, even through the bullshit, how determined we had been to get back on track.

The stories of past failures, parental flaws, relationship woes that he shared made me, caused me to want to take care of him. It was almost like I wanted to heal him. As strong as he fronted to be for his fans, with me, he was the total opposite. He needed to be loved and taken care of. He needed to be accepted one hundred percent fully flawed, and that is what he was grooming me to do. It was what I wanted to do. As independent as he was, he needed a strong woman by his side. Someone who pushed him to greatness, and supported him unconditionally, someone who wouldn't run at the first sign of turmoil. In his words, he was looking for a "best friend to show up and never leave." And here I was…but still.

As all these conversations and statements ran through my head, I began to feel sick to my stomach. What should I do next? Did I go in there and wake his ass up and ask what was going on? Did I throw his shit outside and make him leave? Did I go in there and swing on his ass? Or should I just not say anything? Technically his interactions with those other women had never interfered with how he treated me and had MWB not sent that initial inbox. I would have had no clue, so maybe there was nothing to do but enjoy him for what he was.

At some point, I must have passed out because I remember being awakened by the sound of his narrow feet pitter-pattering down my hallway. Even though I heard him coming, I continued to lay there with my eyes closed as though I was asleep. Within a few moments, I felt him standing over me, not making a sound. I slowly opened my eyes and asked what was wrong? I was paranoid because I did not know if he realized I had been on his phone or not. Was this going to turn into an altercation? On his face, he wore a look that effortlessly combined sadness and exhaustion and quietly said, "Why did you leave me?" I told him I couldn't sleep and hadn't wanted to risk waking him up with my tossing and turning. He thanked me for the consideration but told me next time it was okay if I woke him up; just don't leave him again. He then laid partially on top of me, wrapped his arms around me, buried his head in my chest, and was back to sleep within two to three minutes. That night I do not remember falling asleep.

The next morning, the first thing he did was run to his car. He said he left his shoes and blazer; he would be right back. As soon as the door closed, I raced down the hall to my room and grabbed his phone. There were multiple good morning, I love you, praying for your strengths, hurry homes, and I miss you text messages from an entirely different group of women than those whose messages I read less than eight hours prior. My heart simply sank deeper as I realized there was no way around this situation. I'm not as even-tempered, cool, or calm as I would like to be at my age. The more I thought about the situation, the games, and the lies, the angrier I became. By the time he came back into the house, I was boiling over. I knew I couldn't disclose to him what I knew because then I would have to tell him how I knew it, so instead, I made up a story about MWB messaging me again and telling me of other women. I wanted to see if I dropped specific details would he confess or would he continue to play crazy and deny any wrongdoing on his behalf.

That man looked me right in my eye and reiterated

that MWB was a liar, and she was just mad because I had won. He said there were no other women in his life who mattered but again, that he did have platonic friends, but I had nothing to worry about. For me, nothing was comforting about this moment. This nigga was unstoppable; I could not believe my ears. Not only was he lying, but his ability to look me in the eye with a straight, sincere face and still be lying was sick. The more he lied, the angrier I became. I wanted to tell him so badly that I had gone through the phone and saw all the bullshit, but then the blame would've been on me. I knew exactly how the conversation would have gone; it would become less about what I saw, and the focus would have become the violation of his privacy by going through the phone.

Once he left for the funeral, I blocked him on social media and sent him a text that simply said, "You can't come back here." We exchanged seventy text messages while he was at the funeral, and I still had more to say. It was a combination of arguing, explaining, denying, and flat-out lying; it was so draining. When he came to get his things, initially, he didn't say anything to me. As he rummaged through my room, gathering his belongings, I sat in my living room fuming. I don't know what I expected from him, but it was not for him to act as if he was the one offended or hurt. I guess I expected maybe an apology, a conversation, or something, but he gave me nothing. It wasn't until he was walking out the door that he simply said, "Of all days today, I needed you the most, and this is what you do? You bring all this bullshit to me on the day I buried one of the closest men I had to me. This couldn't have waited?" When what he said registered, I felt torn; perhaps it was inconsiderate, considering the situation, but when would the appropriate time have been? Before or after he gave me an STD or forced me to knock his head off since he insisted on playing with my emotions? There seemed to be no end to the lies, so in my mind, it was now or never. After several moments of silence, he opened my door, looked back at me, and said, "if you want to talk, I'll be at the coffee shop." and left.

Chapter 7

I did not go to the coffee shop. I had projects that needed finishing, and frankly, I was still on the verge of choosing violence. I couldn't stomach seeing him. Once I finished working, I sat and looked back through our pictures, read all our text messages, listened to every voicemail, and watched every video. I saw no signs of unhappiness. Everything we did, he initiated or eagerly went along with, so if I was not truly where he wanted to be, then why was he? I knew I needed to accept the fact that someone I trusted had betrayed me on a level I had never experienced before, but I could not make sense of the how, the why, or the when. We spent a lot of time together, so how had he managing all these other women? I played one voicemail repeatedly. Rightfully so, I was now questioning everything that had taken place between us, and now, instead of savoring his sweet words and the calm melodic sound of his voice embracing the butterflies his words gave me, I was listening for background clues. Where had he when he left this message? Had he been at a chick house hiding in the bathroom? Was he in the car? Had he just gotten out of the bed with someone else the way he had done me so many times to make this call?

Later that evening, I called to check on him and he disclosed that he was on his way back to KC; there was nothing left for him to do here. Plus, his daughter had a game the next day, so he needed to rest.

I asked him to stay.

I wanted to talk (or perhaps argue), and I felt like him leaving had robbed me of that opportunity. I had shit that needed to be said and questions that needed to be answered, and how dare he leave before I was given that chance. He did not get to just walk away without a conversation (or a fight). I wasn't finished. Despite my insistence that he come back to my home, he refused and said he would call me once he made it safely to KC and disconnected the call.

This muthafucka.

Later that night, I called to check on him, mad or not, I needed to know he was okay. The second he answered, I knew two things; 1) he was not back in Kansas City, and 2) he was under the influence. He hadn't been gone long enough to be as intoxicated as he was because under no circumstance did, he drink and drive.

He was still fucking here.

My Yuppie admitted that he hadn't gone home; there was nothing there for him either, so he had stayed. He told me a story about being with his cousins and how he was sitting in his car outside of someone's house on the Southside because he was too fucked up to drive, he was waiting on his cousins because they were headed to the strip club. During this jumbled-up story (that was a complete and total lie, might I add), he made sure to let me know he was mad at me. Even worse, he was disappointed because I was acting like them.... For hours (literally), we went back and forth about what had gone wrong. I still never told him that I had gone through his phone and that it wasn't MWB lying on him...he was just a lie, period. I finally saw for myself.

Eventually, I asked him to come back to my house or at the very least check into a hotel. He did not need to be drunk in the city of St. Louis alone doing anything, let alone anything after midnight. By no definition could my Yuppie be described as a tough guy, so the thought of him drunk in the city alone scared me.

I needed him to be safe.

My Yuppie continued to express his anger and said he would never step foot in my house again. He was fine where he was, and I no longer had to worry about him. I begged him to give me his location, but he told me they were headed to the strip club to bring in his birthday and that he would call me later. Pause. He was not a strip club guy, and outside of brief conversations with these cousins, he didn't hang out with them. And because I had begun to learn his patterns and habits, I knew he would never be willing to venture from the Southside of St. Louis, intoxicated, to East St. Louis to visit a strip club with cousins he didn't hang out with on any other day.

Here he was, lying again.

But after arguing for twelve hours, I had no more fight left in me. If that's the story, he wanted me to believe, cool. Knowing he was alright was good enough for me. That night we stayed on the phone for over four hours before I simply couldn't stay awake anymore. I told him to call me if he needed me.

I woke up at 6:30 AM and when I realized he had not called back, and I panicked. Where had he stayed? Was he safe? Did he make it back from the Eastside? I jumped up, threw on my clothes, and grabbed my keys to go look for him when I realized I had no idea where to begin. I called twice before he finally called back. He said they never went inside the strip club but had sat on the parking lot all night, drinking, smoking, and kicking it. He said he was on his way back to this side but needed me to help him find a place to get a quick oil change before he hit the highway. After finding a spot, I talked to him until he arrived at his location, my nerves were calmed. Well, kind of. I rode past the oil change spot he was at because, at this point, I didn't believe anything that came out of his mouth, and I needed to see him there, alone, although I didn't expect him to be.

I was wrong. I watched for a few minutes as he sat there on his phone, drinking coffee while they serviced his vehicle. I then headed back home and did my best to relax, but my mind would not stop racing. I was back in the space where I questioned myself. Why had I gone through his phone in the first place? How could I be so insensitive to start a fight with him on the day of the funeral, of all days? Would he ever forgive me? Yes, you heard it right. Somehow, I felt bad about the situation. I knew what I had seen but didn't I owe it to him to allow him a chance to explain? What if he was trying to end everything with everyone else, and I had just ruined my chance? Maybe it wasn't as bad as I imagined? I mean, there was no way that anyone else really mattered because he devoted so much time to me and meeting my needs and making sure I was happy...they were just time fillers because I wasn't there.

Had I fucked up?

Eventually, he called and said he was headed my way; it was his forty-seventh birthday and he had to see me before he left. He asked me to draw him a bath and to have the mimosas flowing. I did. Once he arrived, he did not stop to hug or kiss me, he went and got straight into the tub (red flag). Instead of questioning his actions, I followed him in the bathroom and sat on the sink top while he bathed. We didn't talk much, and in all honesty, I was only in there to make sure he didn't call or text anyone. At some point, he asked if I would come home with him...his daughter had games, so there would be periods when he wouldn't be there, but overall, he wanted me with him. I declined his offer because 1) I knew the information that was in his phone, and I was not sure how much longer I could hold my composure, and 2) the next day was Mother's Day—I wanted to be with my child.

Once he finished bathing and was dressed, we drank several mimosas, took some pics, made some boomerangs, and parted ways. But before he did, I publicly acknowledged him on social media, something I had never done before. I posted a copy of the commissioned poem I gifted him for his twentieth anniversary of him being a journalist, pics of us at various events, and a fake ass mushy post—from the outside, it was super sweet and endearing, but in reality,

I had sunk to a new low and only did it to be petty. I have never posted a love interest on social media outside of my kids' dad and my ex-husband...well, Paula's son got a little airtime but outside of them, never. As much of an open book as I am, my children and my romantic relationships are two things I am careful about sharing with the world. In actuality, the only reason I did it was to let them know I was HER. You see, he would never see the sweet messages, the tags, or the pictures; his ass was still blocked, but they would. And that's exactly what I wanted.

With my silly-tail self.

We did not talk one time throughout his three-and-a-half–hour trip. He called to let me know that he made it home and said he was at the mall—he didn't want to go home. He was running on fumes and had been awake for over twenty-four hours. His fear was going home and passing out; he could not miss baby girls' game, so he stayed out until it was time to get her. After that, I didn't give him a second thought. I went about my day, only sharing this newfound information with my then best friend because I needed to tell someone.

The next morning the sound of my phone ringing woke me up out of my sleep, "Good morning, baby," he said. "Good morning, my babe." It was as if nothing I discovered over the past few days mattered. I asked why I hadn't heard from him, and he said after the game he and the kids went and grabbed food, and as soon as he got home, he crashed. He went on to say that he wished I would come and spend the day with him; his birthday had been horrible, and he should have stayed in St. Louis with me. BRIEFLY, I considered going to spend the day with him. If he could forgive me for creating chaos on the day, he lost one of the most important men he had in his life, then surely, I could forgive him for a few text messages, right? I didn't really know the true context behind the messages, and as he had said to me before, you can't control who sends you anything, so maybe, just maybe, he wasn't the monster I painted him to be in my head. Maybe there was still a chance, for him.... for us

We chatted for perhaps five to seven minutes total before the unthinkable happened.

.

An excerpt from my blog, The Biggest Betrayal of All Time (Part I)

Yelling, feet scurrying on a hardwood floor, doors slamming, deep breathing..."Hello," the voice said, "Is this SJ?"

Y'all know how you watch a really bad movie, and you want to turn it off, but you can't; where you know the ending is going to be shitty, but you just HAVE to see it for yourself? Well, that was me for the next twenty-four minutes. This lady, the five-year lady (whom he told me he broke up with in January), informed me that there were no children's games the day prior, but rather they had dinner reservations, and then he stayed at her house. She went on to say how he told her outside of family obligations, his main purpose of being in St. Louis had been to break up with me, that he had called her several times on my watch and that he had invited her to join him in St. Louis.

Now let's pause to fully understand the depths of this shit. How did this man think he was going to

89

be here, in my city, with a whole nother woman? Like, where was he going to tell me he was? What was she going to do while he was with me? How was he going to explain to us not spending the night together? Y'all the shit SO sick in hindsight, but anyway, let me finish.

During our conversation, she proceeded to go through the phone and read numerous texts between him and other women (whom she was simultaneously texting) where he was professing his love, making plans, and every other scumbucket thing imaginable.

Fast forward, twenty-four minutes of an eye-opening convo, threats of violence, one police chase involving an elderly man (his ass), and five hours of talking to him; all was well.

At this point, for me, God had done his job. Things could get no clearer than this, and I was left to deal with the harsh reality that in fewer than thirty days, two women, both my elders, had been granted access to my life because of him. The most important task of ANY man I entertain is to

PROTECT ME, and he had failed miserably. Both of these women had been following me on social media, sending him screenshots of my page...one even went so far as to zoom in on my picture to read the affirmations on my mirror; she asked him if I was pregnant because one of my sticky notes mentioned me wanting to become a mother again...

This nigga...ole babe, my Baby, my Yuppie, my Fly Guy was undoubtedly gonna make me fuck him up. He jokingly called me "his shooter" because I, too, was very transparent about my past, so he knew better...or at least he should have.

*****

Eventually, Queen Sugga gave him his phone back, and he left her home; I called him within minutes. For whatever reason, I wasn't mad, but I damn sure needed an explanation. We ended up talking on the phone for approximately three hours, during which time he told me every variation of the same lie over and over again. My first question was why had he left me to go be with her if they had (per his words) broken up months ago, and why had he used his daughter as a pawn in this

91

game? Why not just be honest? He ran the same line on me that he had with MWB—he and Queen Sugga were friends, and ever since he ended their relationship, she had been highly emotional. He told me because of her inability to have children, Mother's Day was rough for her and that she begged him to spend time with her. I then wanted to know why he had asked me, on multiple occasions, to come home with him if he knew he had plans with her? What if I had said yes? His only response was, then I would have been with you.

During these same three hours, I again experienced him going through every range of emotion known to man. Initially, he was mad at me because I had sat on the phone and allowed "that crazy lady" to talk about him. He couldn't understand why I hadn't hung up. He then transitioned into how much he hated Queen Sugga and how once again, his kindness had been taken for granted. He hadn't wanted to be there with her, he only did it because she needed him, and in turn, this was how she repaid him? He screamed and ranted about her being mad he wouldn't sleep with her and that her true anger came from that fact. She, like MWB, couldn't stand that I had come into the picture and took her place. Based on the one-sided conversation we had, you would have sworn they were enemies.

He was hurt and embarrassed that she had gone through his phone and texted everyone, including professional contacts. And in true my Yuppie fashion, in the blink of an eye, the entire conversation changed. He told me of all the women he had ever dealt with, she had been the most loyal and the one he trusted the most. Now in his eyes, she was just as bad, if not worse, than MWB, and he could never talk to her again; and the thought of that hurt him. He said although he didn't agree with what she had done, the more he thought about it, he understood how she felt and was remorseful.

Again, this was one of those moments where I was able to remove myself from the situation and fully embrace and respect what he was saying. He did owe her a full and genuine apology for putting her in a fucked-up position, and she needed to know that she was not the cause for his behavior. I admired the fact that he wanted to make sure she was ok because, as he said, she had never given him a reason to do any of the things he had done to her over the years, and rightfully so, he felt horrible.

After allowing him to express himself without judgment, once again, he flipped the script and began yelling at me. It was almost as though he was so prepared for me to spazz out he was trying to beat me to the punch. Any small, ridiculous thing he could say to get a reaction out of me, he would say: "It's only been a few months I don't owe you shit!" "Walk the fuck away. I don't give a fuck. I don't even know you." He repeatedly screamed that he didn't give a fuck, because all I had done was show myself to be weak like them, so maybe it was best if I left. Everyone ran when shit got hard, he said, so fuck me forever; I had lied to him about who I was and who I was capable of being to him, and he didn't want anything more to do with me. He called me a liar.

With another blink of an eye, he was apologetic. He was sorry for pulling me into his world when he knew his affairs were not in order. But needed me to know he was trying to clear things up for me, but he didn't want to hurt anyone else. He had invested years with them (MWB and Queen Sugga), so he felt a sense of obligation to them. He had no idea things would get this messy. He reminded me that he came for me. If either of them meant anything to him, there would be no me. He thought ending things with them would be easy. He thought he was in control, but clearly, he underestimated the situation.

By the end of the conversation, I had agreed to spend the following weekend in Kansas City with him. There was a comedy show that Friday he wanted us to attend.

So, at this point, I know everybody reading this is like WHAAAATTTTT!!!! Don't do it!! But let me explain....

For whatever reason, despite knowing everything, I still wanted closure. Fuck that—I NEEDED closure. I knew my Yuppie was not who he represented himself to be, but his saying is true that until a person has reached their limit, nothing no one else says matters. Hell, logic, and common sense don't even matter. Everything in me screamed WALK AWAY before I found myself in a position where I had to stay.

Everything MWB had said out of anger with regards to his character had shown itself to be true; he was a liar, a serial cheater, a manipulator, and a narcissist...but I hadn't had enough yet. I needed to allow him the opportunity to make this situation right. I could never trust him again as a lover, but I didn't want to lose him as a friend. I valued him and our time together. I was a fan first and a lover second...I couldn't lose him. But still, I knew, this had the potential to go wrong. I know myself and everything I'm capable of, and I knew there was no way for this to not end in disaster. Fun SJ fact; I've never re-loved a nigga or re-friended a foe. Once you cross me, don't trust me, I don't mean you any good.

But I couldn't let go.

As sick as it was, I needed to know that our time together, no matter how short, had mattered to him. So that following Friday, I packed my bags and headed to Kansas City to be with him.

Chapter 8

On my way there, I didn't listen to any music or talk on the phone, not even to him. Even though the week had been fine—he was attentive, sent Cash Apps, and apologized far more times than I could count, I knew I was walking into a mess. I knew by showing him that I forgave him not once but twice, things would only get worse, and he would begin to respect me less and less; the same way he did the others. Contrary to what women believe or have been falsely told by men, sticking by a man through indiscretions is one of the fastest ways to ensure that he does it again. Men will say they respect the woman who doesn't run, the ride or die, the through thick and thin chick, but that couldn't be further from the truth. My Yuppie was the definition of "if you give a man an inch, he's going to take a mile…." I mean, look at the situation with MWB. She had been trying to run chicks off to secure her spot and had faithfully and foolishly gone back every single time she caught him with someone, and three years later, she was no closer to being his woman, let alone his wife, than she was the day she met him.

But then there was the connection... it is rare to find a man as charismatic, down for whatever, and full of zest as he was. One who supported you in ways only imagined, that listened to your heart's desires, and one as involved in, connected with, and concerned for the community as he was. Someone with goals, dreams, and aspirations. Someone who overcame every single situation that was meant to stop or destroy him. He was a fighter, an inspiration—he was my inspiration. But still, I knew I had to find the strength to leave. My temper isn't what it used to be, and the mere thought of this man continuing to play with me the way he had been playing with them just didn't sit well in my spirit. This weekend was uncharted territory for me. Never had I been in a space with someone who had committed such egregious crimes of the heart with as many women as he did. And because I know me, I was aware that I was only a comment, inbox, or text message away from inflicting bodily harm on this man. A man whom I adored with my whole heart. For both of our safety, I knew that after that last weekend together, I would never see him again. I promised myself no matter how much it hurt, I would enjoy every single moment and bring up nothing...I hadn't come to argue.

I pulled up at his home around 2:00 PM, the peak of the workday. He was already in the living room working, so I joined right in. Occasionally I looked up from my computer and watched him work. Simultaneously he sent emails, text messages, responded to DMs, worked on his story, which was due at 4:00 PM, all while attending to my needs. One of the things I adored about him is the way he tended to me. Once I completed my work-related tasks, I kissed him on the forehead and headed to his room to lay down.

As soon as my head hit the pillow, I instantly smelled a strange musty smell; it was something I never smelled there before. While his home was modest, to say the least, it was never dirty, so something about this smell struck a nerve. I moved the pillows around, sniffing each one, trying to get a better feel for what it could be, but I couldn't call it. Instead of questioning him, I placed one of my shirts across the pillow, sort of like a pillow covering, and crashed. I'm not sure how long I slept before I felt him creep into the room and whisper in my ear that he had to leave. He was headed to the game and would call me when it was time for me to meet him. A few hours later, when he called asking if I was ready, I jumped up so quickly that I threw my phone off the bed and onto the floor. When I reached down to grab it, something white underneath the bed caught my eye, I reached for it without thinking because whatever it was had a designated place, and that place wasn't under the bed.

When I pulled the white object out and held it up to see what it was, I discovered it was a pair of soiled, small girl's underwear—white. I could not believe my fucking eyes. After every conversation we had this past week, after every promise and every denial, this nigga had still a chick in this damn house, and clearly, they had been fucking, because how else were her panties off? That rage I felt less than a week ago when he was at my house returned. I jumped up to grab my suitcase and head back to St. Louis, this shit was too much. But before I did, I sent him a picture of the panties and said, "Wow, the universe is working against you these days."

It didn't take him long to respond, "It's not. But I'm sorry, and it's not what you think. I can explain." Instead of taking my ass home as I knew I should have, instead, I went in search of alcohol—I needed something to calm my nerves. When I opened the fridge, the first thing I noticed was that it was full of groceries—things he would never buy, and there was a bottle of opened red wine...and he doesn't drink wine.

The chick had been here overnight.

For about forty-five minutes, we went back and forth via text message. I discussed the disappointment and disrespect I felt, and he told me that this woman, who he never named, was yet again a bitter chick that he was breaking things off with, and she left the panties out of spite. She had come over the night before so that they could talk, and she hadn't taken him distancing himself from her very well. He said she had not spent the night, and they didn't have sex.

The rest of the night was horrible. I stayed despite knowing I should have left. Everything he sat, I snapped, I was fed up with all of his bullshit and could no longer hide it. We decided to skip the comedy show and meet at Dodson's Bar & Commons for food and drinks. By the time I arrived, he had already ordered and was sitting at a table facing the street. As I approached, my rage resurfaced once again. The thought of him having slept with someone fewer than twenty-four hours of sleeping with me was a hard pill to swallow. Once again, I felt so betrayed, except this time, there was no one to blame but myself. I knew what he was capable of back in April, so there was no logical reason why I was there. After the meaningless conversation, fake tears (his), and the nastiest attitude I'd had in years, I just wanted to leave. He asked me to chill out and enjoy the weekend; he wanted us to enjoy the weekend he planned, and, come Monday, if I never wanted to talk to him again, he would respect it.

Once we arrived back at his house, I immediately passed out on the smelly-ass bed because where else would I sleep? He sat in the living room, played his records, drank his drink, and had a regular ol' jam session like nothing had happened. I was disgusted. Visions of another woman in his house, in his bed, flooded my dreams. I envisioned another woman in the very spot I laid in, and it made me physically sick to my stomach. But what was there for me to do at this point?

I'm not sure when he came and got in the bed, but when I rolled over and felt him, I immediately jumped up. Not only did I not want to lay next to him, but I needed to get to that phone. I still can't figure out, knowing what he had going on, why there was no lock on his phone. Not only to protect him from chicks like me who had reached their boiling point, but just for privacy purposes in general. He had nudes, sex videos, and everything else under the sun in there, so to not have a lock on it was a sign of arrogance; he never expected anyone to step out of their assigned roles in his life and go against the grain. That's one of the first things he told me when we met—if a woman ever went through his phone, it was an automatic dealbreaker; he would not be violated.

As I scrolled through the phone, I was not shocked to see various messages from multiple women this time. On his birthday Queen Sugga sent him screenshots of my story and wanted to know why I was allowed to post pictures of us, and she wasn't. He had responded by saying, "She's a fool. She knows I love you."

Another chick texted saying there were groceries in the fridge and by the front door—she was too tired to bring them all in. She went on to explain that the snacks in the fridge were for his children and wished him an amazing, fun-filled weekend with them—she would be home Monday when he dropped them off.

Then there was Vivian, who he told he was at Soiree with his homeboys when she called; it was too loud, and he wouldn't have been able to hear her over the noise, but he promised to call once he made it to the car.

Lil baby texted, asking for "her dick." He told her once he finished up his weekend, she would be his first stop.

There was Author Chick, who continuously told him that she loved him and referred to him as her future. She always referred to them as being KCs up-and-coming power couple, to which he replied, "We are, baby. They not ready yet."

There was so much shit in that phone it was crazy. But of everything, the most disturbing thing I saw was an interaction with a woman we will call Kelly for the sake of this book. Kelly was an older (well, at least she looked older) Caucasian female who lived approximately two hours away from KC. They, like everyone else, had met via social media and were transitioning to the next level. He had invited her to the comedy show...yes, you read that right, the very same comedy show I was in town for, and ironically, he had done so while I was on the highway headed to him. I read on as their conversation covered her journey to KC to spend the night with him and as he wished her safe travels. When Kelly arrived that night, he told her that something had come up with his children and he would be unable to attend the comedy show with her. She was disappointed, and rightfully so; she had driven two hours to spend time with him. I continued to read his apologies to her and his promises to make it up to her the next day; he gave a location for him to meet Saturday morning for coffee...all of this while I was there with him.

Those moments when he had been running to his car to grab whatever he was missing were actually spent calling other women. When he would be in the bathroom for two hours getting ready, he was sending nudes, video chatting with women, calling, and texting the others. There was even one woman who he asked to join him in his home (the very home where I was reading all these messages from), and her reply was that she was sorry; she had her kids and couldn't get away. But what if she had said, "Ok, I'm on the way"? I was there, so how would that have worked?

I couldn't go back to sleep that night. I had to pray myself down from pouring boiling water all over his scrawny-ass body because, at that point, I was ready to risk it all. But I knew I needed to keep my composure. My next move had been planned, I had to see this through.

What happened next was the craziest thing I had done throughout this entire situation. Crazier than me forgiving him after MWB inboxed me. Crazier than me agreeing to see him after Brown Sugga snatched the phone out of his hand while we were talking. Even crazier than me turning this situation into two blogs, a roundtable, and a best-selling novel all within four months.

I turned all my emotions off.

Just like that, I went from an emotionally unstable mess to completely placid. I realized that under no circumstances would I risk going to jail for hurting a nigga who couldn't even afford my bail, and at the same time, I knew with 100% certainty that the weekend would not end without this nigga knowing exactly who the fuck I was and why I warned people regularly NOT TO PLAY WITH ME BECAUSE I DIDN'T PLAY FAIR. Fuck fair. In fact, it was a proven SJ fun fact that if you played with me, my emotions, or my children, I was undoubtedly going to take shit too far. I'd prayed to overcome the immaturity that caused me to behave in such a manner, but like many others, my time hadn't come yet. I knew Jesus was still in the business of turning heathens into saints, but apparently, I was still in the back of the line. Every ounce of malicious and vindictiveness in me had been activated.

Chapter 9

By the time he woke up, I was able to go about the day as if nothing ever happened. Not the dirty ass panties I found under the bed and not even the dozens of text message conversations he had on my watch. I did nothing to indicate that anything was amiss, and I planned to keep it that way. That morning he cooked us breakfast, and we immediately settled into our groove. Music blasting, singing, dancing, intimacy...honestly, I can say, this was one of the best times we had together. Maybe because I knew this was the last time, I would see him. Whatever it was, we had an amazing morning.

Around 5:00 PM, we prepared for dinner at Trezo Mare Restaurant & Lounge and enjoyed a delectable steak dinner and cocktails. Something didn't feel right. He couldn't stay off his phone, kept running to the bathroom, and had a constant look of worry and stress on his face. No more was the light, carefree Yuppie that I had the pleasure of experiencing a few short hours ago—something was blowing up in his world, and he was trying his best to address it while entertaining me at the same time.

After dinner, he made reservations for us at a quaint rooftop lounge, the Canary. The sights were beautiful, the drinks were strong, and it was perfect rooftop weather. As the day progressed, I could tell whatever was going wrong in his world had escalated. At one point, I watched him engage in a forty-three-minute (I timed it) text conversation with so much fury and vigor that he started cursing at the phone. For forty-three minutes, he sat across from me in complete silence, he didn't even sip his drink, and he never acknowledged my presence; he had been totally consumed in whatever had been going on. Eventually, he looked up, perhaps he felt me staring at him, or he finally remembered that we were on a date; he asked what was wrong. I told him nothing, I was just waiting on him to wrap up what he was doing so we could enjoy our drinks. He apologized for being distracted, and our night continued. Once we left there, I was genuinely tired, but he said he wasn't ready to go home. Again, strange for him because while he had never told me no about anything I'd ever wanted to do or see, he wasn't really a nightlife type of guy. But he insisted we go on to a third location, a club, which was highly odd behavior for him. It was almost as if he was stalling, he hadn't wanted to go home.

We arrived at Soiree Steak & Oyster, the last stop of the night, a laid-back spot located just east of downtown KC in an area known as 18th and Vine. This historic district is home to the NLB Museum, American Jazz Museum, Kansas City Juke House, and the Ethnic Art Gallery, to name a few. Once we got inside and settled at a table with our drinks, I sat and admired him. Even casual, he was well dressed. His fitted red baseball cap and red converse perfectly complemented his all-black attire topped with a soft black leather slim-fit jacket. He made forty-seven look good in ways unspoken. It was his aroma, the way his head was never fully clean-shaven but the after shadow fit his rustic appearance perfectly. The slight curve in his fingernails, the crock in his teeth, the freckles on his face... I was going to miss him so much. I knew my next move would sever any opportunity we had left to remain friends, and the thought made me sad. But I knew I had to save myself...not from him, but from me. Although I knew exactly what he was capable of and that the guy I had fallen for didn't exist, he was still my person. It was him I called when I had a business question, him I called when I wanted to attend an event, him I called when shit in my family hit the fan; when I wanted to laugh or felt like crying, it had all been him, and now I was losing him forever.

Now what?

Against the wishes of my heart, my mind was made up. I knew what needed to be done. After fighting for years to free me from the emotional bondage, a failed relationship had placed me in, under no circumstances would I ever voluntarily send myself back to that place. As I watched him text with other women and run to the bathroom every forty-five minutes, undoubtedly, to talk to them, I simply smiled as I re-read the note I had worked on off and on throughout the day on my phone. You see, during dinner earlier that night, I started composing a message designed to be sent out to every woman I saw in his phone. My intention was not to bully or hurt anyone the way MWB had done with me but to provide them with solid evidence of what had been going on to at least afford them the opportunity to make an informed decision about their relationship with him. I knew I only had one shot to give them as much information as possible, so I had read and reread the message at least ten times to ensure nothing important had been left out.

"Who the fuck are you texting?" he screamed at me over the music; I hadn't noticed him return to the table. I looked up in confusion only to see him staring at me, frowning. "You've been on your fucking phone all night. Who the fuck are you talking to?" Startled by his tone and audacity, I said nothing initially, then quietly muttered, that it had been my son, and I apologized for not giving him my full attention. The irony of him being upset that I had been on my phone did not escape me. Not only was he self-projecting, but he was trying to fake a fallout; there must have been somewhere else he needed to be. Instead of falling for the bait, I ordered us another round of drinks and continued to rock to the sounds of the live band until the lights came on.

We headed to the house.

That night was the most restless night I had ever experienced while in his presence. I felt him constantly moving, up and down all night long. In and out of the bed, from the bedroom to the bathroom multiple times, down the stairs, to the living room, back to the bathroom, in the bedroom (checking to see if I was awake), outside to his car...at one point I even smelled him baking fresh cookies. I laid there silently, never giving him any indication that I was awake, not even when I heard him talking to a woman making plans to see her Sunday morning for brunch.

At 6:00 AM, May 16th, I jumped up and started quietly moving my bags to the car. When I finished, I woke him up and told him I was going to head out. He questioned why I needed to leave so early (despite having a brunch date scheduled with someone else) and why I couldn't stay with him. I explained the forecast predicted heavy rain, and I did not want to get caught in the storm. For the next hour, I loved on him. I sat fully clothed next to his naked body, touching him and soaking in his essence. The smoothness of his beautiful mocha-colored skin. Those soft full lips that so eloquently allowed every lie known to man to flow from them, but that also did amazingly nasty things to me. I carefully traced over the scars he explained had been inflicted by a friend. I kissed him all over his face and told him how much I enjoyed our weekend together and how glad I was to have shared his space. At one point, he jokingly said, "Damn, you act like you're never going to see me again." I didn't respond, just smiled, and continued to soak him in.

One final kiss and I told him there was no need to see me out; I would call him shortly.

I quickly grabbed the last of my belongings, including his cellphone and left.

Stealing [ˈstēliNG] NOUN—the action or offense of taking another person's property without permission or legal right and without intending to return it, theft. (Webster's Dictionary)

Yes, you read that correctly: I left his home with not only my belongings but his as well. Now be mindful, per the verified definition listed above, I hadn't stolen his phone, regardless of what he wanted everyone to believe; I had every intention of returning it once my mission was complete. So instead of saying I stole the phone, I'd like to think of it more as borrowing...yeah, that's it, I borrowed his phone for a few hours; nothing more and nothing less.

Only a few minutes passed before he started calling my phone through Facebook messenger and sending messages. I quickly pulled into my pre-planned location, a church around the corner from his home, turned off the location on his phone, and hit the send button on the message I had sent from my phone to his; the message went out to the thirteen women he was currently in relationships with.

Hey y'all, hey. This is SJ (my Yuppie's) STL girlfriend. I'm sure many of you got the text last weekend from his KC girlfriend, Queen Sugga, so I figured I'd keep the party going since our bae can stop lying. Two women have messaged me about this man, and I've ignored it all because we've only been dating since January. I made myself believe it didn't matter. And we are building. I thought a long-distance situation where you still manage ten to twelve days a month together and talking for five to six hours daily was headed in the right direction. I assumed the other women were lying because how could he have the time. Anywho, I am currently at his house. I've been here since Friday morning (I came for the comedy show), so anyone who doubts what I'm saying is free to join us. I am currently texting thirteen ladies who My Yuppie has seen or asked to see in the last five days. His ability to juggle us all and all of these stories is crazy. But from the lady who left her white panties here Thursday. The lady he offered to take to the comedy show. The lady who bought the groceries here (his kids are NOT here honey, he just knows I like snacks, thank you especially for the Core, it's my favorite). **Author Chick, he called you his future, ma'am...him and his mama talked to Queen Sugga last week and said that she was going to be his wife, so be safe. I'm sure that's not the power couple dynamic you were thinking. Now Vivan, you might be good. He lied to you about Soiree Friday, we did that last night, but besides that, you seem to get more honesty than the rest of us. I'm not sending this because he's breaking up with me. That seems to be what he tells everyone: "These bitches don't know how to walk away." We've had an amazing time. Friday was rough, but Saturday, we had 6:00 PM reservations at Trezo Mare, 8:00 PM reservations at the Canary, stopped by a new coffee shop, and ended the night at Soiree. We spent the whole morning dancing, drinking, singing, and planning future business moves. I was ok with all of his lies until I realized that even on our breaks from intimacy, he was texting y'all every chance he got. I'm not telling anyone what to do. My dumb ass still fucked with him after I knew, so I'm not in the position. But I did want to clarify the lies. And no, he did not come to St. Louis last weekend to** break up with me. We celebrated his birthday Thursday before the funeral (we were scheduled for Louisville), and he went home Saturday. He told me his daughter had a game, but the truth was Queen Sugga was taking him to dinner at 6:00 PM. Fast forward to 8:00 AM Sunday. He calls me from her house, and she snatches the phone, bam group text goes out from his "KC girlfriend." He asked me to come last Sunday because he didn't feel celebrated on his birthday, but I didn't. This fun-filled weekend was his way of apologizing. My Yuppie has NEVER mentioned us breaking up. But we have talked about babies and me moving to KC. We've looked at places. My Yuppie and I are not on bad terms. We are not beefing. He doesn't even know I know about ALL of y'all. So do what you may with the information. I'm not being mean or accusatory like the women who texted me. I am truly just letting y'all know. He's a great guy, fun, sex amazing, and professionally dope as fuck. It's that other shit you gotta worry about. Lastly, Queen Sugga, if you think me and MWB are loud, you should meet some of his other chicks..and while you're busy sending him

screenshots of my post, spend that same energy figuring out why after five years, you've never even lived with that man. Why he's on vacation with a new bitch every month on your watch. Why he can't stay outta St. Louis or perhaps why he was ready to risk his relationship with you for me and the other 'loud, ghetto bitches'...perhaps spice it up a bit, ma, 'cause based on his roster, you aren't EVEN his type, you're just loyal and dumb. And I'm ONLY saying this because after listening to you for twenty minutes last week, respectfully, understanding your plight, I even accepted your apology...you still went on to talk shit about me, and I've done nothing to you. Typical silly-ass woman.

(The exact text message sent — Intimate details and real names were omitted for privacy purposes)

Chapter 10

For the next two and a half hours, I talked to seven women and texted with even more. As the true depths of his sickness were revealed, I sat in my car in total shock and disbelief. The first person I spoke to revealed herself to be my Yuppie's girlfriend of four years; I'll call her Auntie. This older woman was very calm, but you could hear the heart break in her voice. The first thing she said to me was, "Is this all true? Please don't lie to me." For at least an hour, I listened to her tell a tale of meeting this amazing guy and this amazing whirlwind relationship she quickly found herself in. Early on, at his suggestion, they had STD testing conducted and had not used protection since; she had been one hundred percent monogamous throughout their relationship, and although she had her suspicions, he told her he was too. That was her man, she believed him. What struck me as odd about her was that although I remembered him telling me details about her, no one knew that there was a four-year chick; somehow, he had managed to keep her away from everybody and everything. She said that in the beginning, she and my Yuppie traveled a lot, and she had been to St. Louis with him on several occasions and had even met his mom. In fact, she had also been invited to the funeral, and when she declined, they spent Thursday morning, before he came to my house, together intimately. Lately, she described their relationship as shaky, saying it had been for the past few months. She had received the text message from Queen Sugga on Mother's Day, and when she confronted him about it, he told her his phone had been stolen and he didn't know who sent that message. She was shocked when it came because they had been together several times that week, and he promised her things would change between them; he didn't want to lose her. Auntie revealed that she knew about MWB and had heard of Queen Sugga but had been told that both of those relationships were over; she had no idea I existed.

As the messages and the phone calls continued, I

shrank more and more inside of myself. I realized that sending this message was the best thing I could have ever done for multiple reasons; but mainly because I would have never known any of this was going on had I not. I genuinely thought MWB and Queen Sugga were the only people I had to "worry" about, and it wasn't because he was interested in continuing relationships with them but because they had history. I had no idea that there were weeks when he was having unprotected sex with different women every day, sometimes two women a day, or that he would on occasion spend the morning with one woman at his home (intimately), leave her there, go spend the afternoon (more intimacy) with another and return home to the first woman that evening. All of the days and the women overlapped with one common theme, except for MWB, all of these women, me included, were sexually exclusive with only him.

He had the game and was gone with it.

I listened to women explain how they had taken the Plan B pill multiple times, he refused to use protection with certain women and although they loved him, they knew something was off so they refused to bring children into the mess. He had been going on lunch and dinner dates nearly every day, and the same attention he had given me, he had given them simply in other ways. For me, working from home at my own pace allowed me the freedom to text, talk, or video chat throughout the day. Because he engaged in those activities with me all day, every day, I assumed I was special. Since everyone's situation was so different, he simply mastered the art of adapting to the needs of all of his women. Everyone always got exactly what they needed from him.

He was just that good.

I received a text from a Caucasian woman who said, "Lol, another one? He is sick of you bitches and your childish ways. Guess that's why he has me." This is the same chick that, in response to Queen Sugga's text, had sent a full-frontal nude and said that she could care less about what he did with anyone else, as long as he was good to her.

By this point, I'd had enough. There were so many pictures, videos, messages, and just as many inboxes across various social media platforms; my Yuppie had been busy.

He continued to call me via Facebook, he wanted me to know that he reported the phone stolen, and his next step was to call the police and report a theft. His concern was not the women I had contacted, but he needed his phone; his children needed to be able to get in touch with him. Just as I was telling him I would be his way shortly; Queen Sugga called.

She had received my message via Facebook but had no idea what was going on; she had blocked him and hadn't talked to him in a few days, even though he had been emailing her daily. I explained everything that had taken place, and we both sat in silence suppressing tears. Eventually, I spoke, I told her I was sorry for hurting her. I needed everyone to know what was going on but hoped I hadn't hurt her in the process; I know I did though. She then apologized for the messages I saw from her about me, and she said that my Yuppie had told her so many things about me and my actions, she viewed me as the enemy. He told her I would not leave him alone; I was mad that he had broken up with me, and now I was harassing him, and she would be next. The reason she had declined his invitation to the funeral was that she did not want the confrontation with me. When I told her about Auntie and that she had also been invited to the funeral, she simply chuckled and said that sounded about right.

The stories she shared with me were an exact replica of what was taking place now. When she met him five years ago, he told her he was in a situation, but if she gave him ninety days, and it would be taken care of. Of course, it never was. She endured countless confrontations with other women, had caught him in more lies than she could count, had received inboxes from various women and informed me that she and MWB had a couple of run-ins previously.

The only thing I wanted to know from her was when he called me from her house on Mother's Day, how did he get there? Because the story he gave me was that his baby had a game and afterward, he went home and crashed. Come to find out, there had not been a basketball game that weekend at all. He had gone home because they had 6:00 PM dinner reservations at

Firebirds Wood Fired Grilled, and afterward, they spent the night at her house. According to her he begged her to spend his birthday with him, he couldn't imagine not spending it with her, and now that we were officially separated, he wanted to celebrate. She said the whole week leading up to that day he had been telling her that my stalking and harassing had become too much for him to handle. He described a version of me that I didn't recognize—a chick completely obsessed with the thought of being with him that I refused to take no for an answer. That even when he asked me not to call him, I continued to do so and that he had been the one to block me on social media. She denied they were intimate on his birthday but said it was not due to lack of effort on his end. She said he tried for hours, and when she continued to deny him, he went and slept on the couch on the lower level at her home.

Pause again...so this meant, based on everything I'd gathered so far, that every day that week he had sex with his live-in girlfriend, had sex Auntie on Thursday morning, me on Thursday evening, and Saturday morning, and he still tried to have sex with Queen Sugga Saturday night. Oh, and let's not forget no one has any idea where he truly was or who he was with Friday night; dude was insatiable.

Queen Sugga went on to say she recalled hearing him downstairs talking on the phone and going in and out of her front door to his vehicle, but it was something about him being on the phone Sunday morning that caused her to spring into action. She admitted she had never touched his phone before, so grabbing it, running, and locking herself in the bathroom was something she never envisioned herself doing, but she had finally been pushed to the edge.

I was speechless.

As I headed to his home to return his phone, one of my best friends called asking what was going on; my Yuppie had sent her a message on Facebook saying I had stolen his phone and that if I wasn't back soon, he would be calling the police. Next, I received a call from another friend saying while scrolling through her timeline, a post on my business page popped up and caught her eye. My Yuppie had made a post calling me a devil and a thief and informed my clients I would soon be in jail, so they shouldn't expect to hear from me anytime soon. Before I could even hang up, another friend texted, reporting the same thing.

I called him through messenger because I had to know why he would involve my professional business in this personal bullshit we had going on. His going on my professional page was a slap in the face because despite having his phone and access to his everything unsavory in it, I never thought to cross that line. Easily I could have gone on his social media platforms and informed his followers that instead of this humanitarian and pillar of black excellence he portrayed himself to be, this mentor and role model, he was no more than a spineless ass old creep who preyed on the vulnerabilities of successful and young women. That he was no more fit to mentor young boys than the dope dealer in the neighborhood—although, in different manners, they both destroyed everything around them with little regard for the consequences so long as their needs were fulfilled. I could have shared the sexual escapades he participated in, the nudes…I had so much at my fingertips but, because I still respected him as a professional, I would have never done that to him.

He had gone too far.

He continued to yell at me, insisting I bring his phone back. So what he had lied about being faithful, could he be thrown in jail for "fucking a lot of bitches" and that what he did in his personal life had no bearing on who he was as a professional and public figure.

Thing is, it did.

I've yet to meet an individual without flaw—everyone has their fair share of them, self-included, and we all make mistakes. But what he was doing was not a mistake. He was intentionally hurting those closest to him. During the day, he was a voice for the soft-spoken. He stood in the gaps for those who couldn't stand for themselves. He was a provider of goodwill. He displayed just enough about his life to emotionally draw you in but never enough for you to truly know him. He was a self-appointed protector of the people. But who was supposed to protect women from the likes of him?

Most of the women involved with my Yuppie were good people, and they lived the life he faked. They were successful, educated, business owners, amazing parents, and all beautifully broken on the inside in some way. He knew because of their professional and sometimes community standing, no one would ever out him or publicly acknowledge what had taken place; they all had too much to lose. So instead, to protect their image, they had to protect him, and that is how he had been able to move the way he had for so many years.

Eventually, I made my way back to his home to drop the phone off. I did not get out of my car, I no longer had the strength to face him. Instead, I sent a message through social media letting him know to come outside, tossed the phone in the grass, and headed back to St. Louis.

Although we both actively checked each other's social media pages, we did not communicate, there was nothing more to be said. My mission had been accomplished, and he surely hated me because how could he not?

On May 25th, a little over a week since the incident happened, I released the first of a two-part blog, *The Biggest Betrayal of All Time*. Up until that moment, no one except a few close friends knew what transpired. It took my first blog over twenty-four hours to hit one thousand page views, but this blog was different. Within hours the messages, inboxes, and phone calls started coming in. People were sharing the blog post everywhere, and within twelve hours, it had surpassed well over one thousand views. Women were thanking me for having the courage to share my story, and men were apologizing, they too had been my Yuppie at some point in their lives. I was receiving messages from people everywhere who had stumbled across the blog and, subsequently, my page. Most of the feedback received had been positive and encouraging, but I received my fair share of criticism as well. I was sharing too much, what happened between him, and I was nobody's business, and I looked like a fool talking about it. I took everything everyone said and took it in but still, I had no regrets about the blog or anything I shared; my truth is just that, my truth, and that was not dependent on anyone else's opinion.

As the days passed, I expected to hear from him. He followed me too closely on social media to have not seen the blog but nothing, not a call, a text, or anything.

Friday of that week, I woke up to everything related to the blog being reported as harassment on my social media site and was placed in FB jail for thirty days. Although one of my friends quickly made a backup page for me to continue promoting my blog, I was annoyed. I knew my Yuppie himself had not taken the time to report my page, but I was one hundred percent sure that it was someone associated with him who had; to this day, my money is still on MWB being the culprit.

My rebuttal to my page being blocked was to produce a roundtable discussing the blog. On June 4th, myself and a few others spent two and a half hours via FB and IG live, discussing part one of the blog and the situation in general. At the beginning of the segment, I told my panel and the viewers that under no circumstance would I tolerate any blatant slander about this man, we would stick to the facts, and that no one would use the real names of anyone involved, not even his.

The conversation was amazing, and the viewer engagement was through the roof. At the end of the roundtable, I announced I would be releasing part two of the blog and the full-length version of this incident in my third book, *The Uglier Side of The Truth*. Not only was the story inspired by my Yuppie so was the book cover and the title. For the last five years, he struggled with wanting to write a novel based on the ugly truths in his life, but fear of public retaliation and concerned about the effect it could possibly have on his career, so the process had stalled.... As my way of paying homage to him, I created my version of his story for him. I told my viewers live that all I needed was ninety days to turn this vision into a reality. People told me there was no way I could write and self-publish a book in that amount of time and that I was crazy for thinking I could.

The book was completed in eighteen days and released seventy-eight days later.

A week or so after the roundtable aired, my Yuppie finally called. He was displeased with what he had been reading on social media and wanted to talk. He apologized again for hurting me and bringing me into his mess, and I apologized for hurting and/or embarrassing him. He admitted to both reading the blog and watching the roundtable and took offense to how he was being portrayed. He didn't want to argue with me and simply wanted the madness to stop. He was concerned about his career and children. What if his children got their hands on the blog? How would they view him? He said he understood the situation had now become a business, but he asked me to please remove his name from any current or future publications and to stop doing side-by-side comparisons of our book covers (they are nearly identical). I agreed to both.

We ended the call with the hopes of a future friendship.

That Monday morning, I received an inbox from a young lady asking me to call her. She said she had received text messages from both Queen Sugga and I and needed to talk; she provided me with her contact information. She wasn't the first female who reached out to me who had been involved in this situation, so there was nothing out of the ordinary about her message. I called the number provided a few minutes later and spoke with SW2020. She had so much to tell me but, most importantly, wanted to warn me that my Yuppie asked her to release some potentially damaging information about me, and she was having second thoughts. He had shared with her my arrest record, personal details I shared with him about my marriage, and personal issues involving my son; he wanted her to expose me. She sent me text messages of him coaching her on what to say and key phrases to use to trigger me. In fact, she said when he called me Saturday night, she was there and that she lived there; he asked her to move in mid-April; right when his behavior began to change.

The more she spoke, I became nauseated. Just when I assumed he had reached the lowest of his low, and couldn't go any lower, here comes this mess. SW2020 knew all about me, but the same as with Queen Sugga and MWB, I was described as just another old, scorned bitch who wouldn't let go. (Old to her—she was under 35 years old.) She told me that she and my Yuppie were in love and planned to have children. She filled in so many missing pieces to this puzzle—those were her panties I had found underneath the bed. The nightgown I left that he

135

couldn't find, she had thrown away; she described it down to the scent. The makeup left smeared on the wall, the eyelash applicator in the bathroom, the extra toothbrush; she knew exactly when I had been in her home. She was literally the missing piece to everything. Once again, I found myself upset; why had he called me Saturday night if he knew this was his plan?

Here I was doing my best to protect his image while still telling my story, and he had intentionally put a plan in place to ruin mine.

I cried.

It was the first real cry I'd allowed myself to have throughout this whole ordeal. I cried as I listened to this young woman describe how he had manipulated her and put her in a situation she was unsure of how to remove herself from. The way he had locked in on her weaknesses and insecurities and used them to his advantage. I cried in fear as I thought of all the women he had slept with unprotected while sleeping with me.

I tried to hold my composure, after all, she lived

with him and the last thing I wanted to do was put her in harm's way; but I simply couldn't contain myself. I called and cursed his ass out. I couldn't believe that just as the dust was settling, he would do such a thing to me. I knew of his past, the undesirable things he had not only shared but others, things I dug up on my own; I was a former Police Officer, I have the right connections to find out damn near anything. There were certain things I hadn't touched and promised I wouldn't because I didn't want his children affected and neither did I. Not one of his eight deserved to find out the truth about their father through a public platform. I also wanted to protect his career—the work he did for the community was much needed, and being the youngest African American in his role, there was always someone looking for a reason to slander his name; I did not want to be the one to give it to them Of course, he denied the entire story and insisted that MWB had spoofed his phone and she was the blame for everything. As I screamed, cursed, and cried from the pit of my soul at this betrayal and he comforted and reassured me that he would never do such a thing, he was also texting SW2020, congratulating her on bringing me to my knees. He boasted about me crying on the phone and having a breakdown. He told her she was good, really good, and he couldn't wait to talk more when they got home.

She sent me everything.

Through a series of unfortunate events, by Wednesday, he realized that she and I had been talking and called to apologize. He asked me to give him a few days to figure some things out, and then he wanted us to have a real conversation—he needed to clear the air once and for all. Initially, I agreed, then decided that closure from this situation wasn't what I needed. I simply needed to be out of it. And the more I prolonged the inevitable, the harder it would be and the more it would hurt as things continued to be exposed. I asked him not to call me again.

He lost it.

So, I thought I was going to expose the world to his private business and then just walk away? Why hadn't I told everybody about getting beat up on the side of the road (never happened), or about the

138

abortions I'd had or the baby that died on my watch when I was a Case Manager? The most UN-tough guy I know was now a raging fake ass gangsta. I listened for thirty minutes as he disrespected me in every way humanly possible before I finally responded. Soon the verbal unpleasantries turned to threats of physical violence and I knew it had gone too far.

The blog and the roundtable were, at best messy, but they were never intended to cause anyone actual harm. Yes, I knew he would be upset, and his already fragile ego would be damaged, but I expected no more than that; hurt feelings. But when my psychic, the same psychic that described him to me with full accuracy, weeks before I met him, told me to be careful, I became worried. She told me he was very unstable and that although he wouldn't have the courage to do anything to me, he had plenty of women waiting and willing to do his dirty work.

I had cameras installed to cover my vehicles and the entryway to my home immediately.

That was the last time I had a two-way conversation with my Yuppie, and I hope it remains that way. I no longer feel anything other than gratitude toward him and everything that happened. After four rounds of STD testing and a ninety-day detox, I'm better; much better. The blog gets new page views daily, as do the roundtable, and the book is set to do numbers. My presale goal is fifty copies, and my end-of-year goal is one thousand; there is no doubt in my mind I will reach both. I am back to my peaceful place, and life is good. That isn't to say I don't have moments where I hear a song or ride past a coffee shop and think about him. As I plan my relocation, it crosses my mind that my move should have been to KC, not clear across the country.

A few weeks ago, MWB began bothering me on social media again. She was back watching my IG stories through a fake page even though I cannot figure out why. I always know when it's her; I'm not interesting enough for fake followers; I'm convinced she is just addicted to drama and toxicity. Our cycle is as such; she starts watching my page, I publicly embarrass her (because I won't be bullied or bothered), she retreats, my Yuppie soups her up to come for me again (cause he's always the force behind the bullshit),

I embarrass her ass worse than before, she retreats again and round and round we go.

I don't know what her end game in to constantly bothering me other than to show her "man" she is rocking with him through babies, foolery and foolishness. I am the queen of transparency—everything in my life is an open book except for my children and my romantic relationships; this situation was the exception. Because of that, there is nothing about me that can ever be exposed, it's already been disclosed. Bankruptcies, abortions, miscarriages, arrests, deaths, near homelessness, domestic violence, you name it, I promise you I've already shared. Why would someone who has built an entire brand on lies and walks around promoting a life that could be no further from their actual reality play this game with a person like me? I was sent pictures and videos that had the power to create enough public discomfort that both of their careers would be over in the blink of an eye. Hell, I have inside information that would strip them both from any level of public credibility ...so why? Of all people, why me?

But still, in true goofy girl fashion, MWB continues to do things like add one of my friends to her close friend's list on IG; she needed me to know they were back together, that toxic love had won. On day 25 of my series, *31 days of SJ*, I jokingly solicited prayers from my followers, they were trying me, and as I mentioned before, God had not finished his work in my heart, I felt a full-blown set of shenanigans brewing. But it was when I was sent the screen recording of her doing a video specifically for me by one of my KC allies that I completely lost it. In the video, she showed them walking through town and her saying that the video was intended to prove a point, they were good. Day 26 of *31 days of SJ* was dedicated to them...cause, again, I always take things too far.

I haven't been bothered since.

I still cannot figure out what the fascination with me is. I know I've been replaced five times over by now, not to mention, word on the street is that he welcomed a new child into the world recently. I have not called, texted, or attempted to reach out to this man since we last communicated in July, and on top of all of that, I am the one who walked away. My Yuppie would have never stopped talking to me. He was accustomed to toxicity; we would have easily fallen into the same pattern he had with everyone else had I allowed it. There were so many more important issues I felt she could be focused on, but instead, she chose me. Kinda cute but high-key creepy.

This book, for me, is the final chapter in this saga. There is nothing left to be said. I walked away unscathed from this situation, outside of hurt feelings, but other women aren't so lucky.

My life lesson in this is to never again ignore the red flags and absolutely believe a man when he says he ain't shit; if he had never been faithful to a woman in twenty-five years, nothing in me should have believed he would change for me. I wanted him to be better and do better, for me and for us but I now know, a leopard doesn't change its stripes and a nigga doesn't change his hoeing-especially not when there are fools who allow it.

143

Narcissistic partners usually have difficulty loving someone else because they don't truly love themselves. They are so focused on themselves that they cannot really "see" their partner as a separate person. Narcissists have inflated self-esteem and are usually very fragile. For these people, even slight criticism can be a narcissistic injury, leading to an angry outburst and desperate attempts to regain their fragile, inflated self-esteem. Narcissistic partners can be very captivating, especially in the beginning. They can make you feel that you too must be great for them to choose you. Grandiose narcissists display high levels of grandiosity, aggression and dominance. They tend to be more confident and less sensitive. They are often elitists and have no problem telling everyone how great they are. Grandiose narcissists are more likely to openly engage in infidelity or leave their partners abruptly if they feel that they are not getting the special treatment that they think they are entitled to.

(PSYCHALIVE, In a relationship with a narcissist? What you need to know about narcissistic relationships._By Lisa Firestone, Ph.D.)